"Hawa has a beautiful way of weaving together food and emotions through stories, and it shows in *Setting a Place for Us*. This is far more than a cookbook; it is a journey of healing against a backdrop of unfathomable loss and chaos. I have learned and felt something new with each chapter, between the essential historical context of each place and the thoughtful care Hawa has put into capturing each recipe. The love and hope carried within this book are palpable, and I know I'll be returning to it time and time again."

—Jenny Dorsey, chef, educator, and executive director of Studio ATAO

"Displacement is not a choice—no one chooses to leave their lands. They're kicked out from them, or they've run away from death and injustice. Even when displaced peoples are far from their homes, the one place to gather and find community is around the table. In *Setting a Place for Us,* Hawa beautifully pays tribute to these people, their stories, and the recipes that bring them together."

—Kamal Mouzawak, founder of Souk El Tayeb

"I love *Setting a Place for Us*! It made me cry, it made me laugh, and it reminded me of the magical importance of food in bringing home to our lives even in exile. This book brings to life senses and emotions to the experience of displacement, wars, and resilience indeed."

—Zainab Salbi, author and founder of Women for Women International and Daughters for Earth

Setting a
Place for Us

For my husband, Kwame Apraku,
"If the sun refused to shine, I would still be
loving you. When mountains crumble to the sea,
there will still be you and me."

This book is dedicated to you and to everyone
like us who has searched the world for a
sense of home and found it within each
other. Thank you for being the best traveler,
storyteller, cook, and friend. I love you.

HAWA HASSAN

Setting a
PLACE
for Us

Recipes and Stories of Displacement, Resilience,
and Community from Eight Countries Impacted by War

Location photography by Mahab Azizi, Riley Dengler, Aline Deschamps,
Doaa Elkady, Omer Khan, Belal Mostamand, and Somaya Samawi
Food photography by Julia Gartland

TEN SPEED PRESS
California | New York

CONTENTS

INTRODUCTION

**MOGADISHU, SOMALIA
1990**

The year is 1990. The air is thick with the putrid smell of burning tires, and the crack of gunfire echoes in the distance. I am four years old, and the city of my childhood is no longer a bustling and burgeoning metropolis but a vacant and violent war zone. Gone are the weekends my family would spend together along the coastline when I would play with my awoowe (grandfather) in the grainy sand. No longer do the nights of gathering to sip tea exist. Instead, we're living in constant fear and uncertainty. Many families like mine are strategizing on how to flee the country as it teeters on the brink of nothingness.

**NAIROBI, KENYA
1991**

By 1991, the fighting had escalated to total civil war and an entire collapse of the state. My hooyo (mother) has taken us, her four children and nine months pregnant with her fifth, across the Kenyan border to the UN refugee camp.

I am five years old, and we are living in the Dadaab refugee camp. My siblings and I spend our days running around the tents while our mother sets up a goods store. She stocks it with rice, flour, beans, and cooking oil as well as canned goods and other packaged food items, and we help her unpack the boxes and line the shelves each day.

Our fellow camp mates come into the store. They ask her for rice, pasta, and clean water and for daily updates about Mogadishu. Despite these difficulties, we are a vibrant community, united by the experience of displacement and the search for safety and security. While our camp residents face significant challenges, they are also a testament

to the resilience and strength of the human spirit in the face of adversity. This is when I learn what grace looks like.

SEATTLE, WASHINGTON
1993

When I'm seven, my mother decides that I should move to Seattle to live with a family friend. "You will have more opportunities," she tells me in our apartment in Nairobi, a place she was able to afford to rent with the money from her goods store. Though I am her second eldest child, I am still too young to disagree with her.

My family waves as I board the flight from Nairobi to New York. From there I will fly to Seattle. In my new home, snow is falling all around me in soft, wet flakes. They carpet the streets and land on my cheek, like a gentle kiss. It's silly, but the snow feels like a promise: my life will now be completely different from my one before, far from the uncertainty and constant fighting.

I start school at Tops Elementary, join the basketball team, and learn English. I'm excited, but soon I feel a deep sense of homesickness. I miss cooking canjeero, bariis, and pasta with my mother. I long to boss my young siblings around again. My big new world seems like an empty dream. I feel angry at everything around me. I can't believe I'm supposed to start over alone.

My mother calls often, and we have pep talks about things I should expect from people or how to get things done. I feel prepared at a very young age. My mother was brave and strong, and I knew I had to be, too. I throw myself into my new world, surrounding myself with people who share my drive and determination.

OSLO, NORWAY
2008

Fifteen years after moving to America, I finally reunite with my hooyo and siblings. Unable to receive their travel documents to join me, they stayed an extra seven years in Kenya before relocating to Oslo.

In the intervening years, my mother has remarried and had five more children, bringing my total number of siblings to nine. She has opened a furniture store and a Somali goods store. She primarily sells traditional Somali clothing and accessories, such as dresses, headscarves, and jewelry. Meanwhile, I have been discovered by a modeling scout while attending college in Seattle. I will go on to live in New York City for nearly two decades and travel the world.

OSLO, NORWAY
2014

I return to Oslo from New York looking for myself, wanting to reconnect the dots of my life. It is the first time I've lived with my mother since I was seven years old, and I'm right back there again as my little-girl self. There's tension between us because she wants me to be that small child and I'm a fully actualized adult with a career and a life. Bubbling up to the surface that hot summer is the clarity of abandonment I've felt over the past twenty-one years, as though I'd been left and forgotten. I realize then that I can't have been the only one who's been on that winding road of displacement. But why don't I know others who've traveled similar paths? Where are our stories? This is the moment I know I will tell these big stories, and I will tell them through food, which is a perfect Trojan horse and a welcoming gateway into culture. Food is both a record of the upheaval of wartime and a comforting talisman of where you've come from and who you are. It's the tie that binds you to your people wherever they are in the world.

BROOKLYN, NEW YORK
2023

I've spent the last year traveling across the world to document stories and collect recipes. It will have taken a decade for me to realize the vision I had on that revelatory trip to Norway. In those ten years, the world has witnessed only more violence and strife. People are still living in wartime conditions, and as my family did all those years ago, they're still leaving their homes and crossing borders. Through it all, they continue to hold their families, friends, and memories together with food.

That's why this book exists: to show you how we who experience violent or invasive conflict in our communities and daily lives are more than our travails. We are who we choose to be no matter what life throws at us. As Warsan Shire, the Somali British poet, says, "No one leaves home unless home is the mouth of a shark." Time and time again, I have seen and experienced that when people live in the mouth of the shark, when blood is in the water, what ultimately surfaces is gratitude, family, community, connection, and togetherness. And it's usually expressed through food or a meal of some kind.

When I first embarked on this book, my intention was to visit all eight featured countries—Afghanistan, Democratic Republic of Congo, Egypt, El Salvador, Iraq, Lebanon, Liberia, and Yemen—to conduct interviews, sample local cuisine, and delve into how these nations preserve their cultural heritage through food and recipes. Sadly, due to COVID-19 and safety concerns, I was unable to travel to all the countries included in the book.

The eight countries I focus on not only boast diverse cultures, histories, and cuisines, but they also share some commonalities. One of the most significant is the impact of historical events such as wars, colonialism, and geopolitical conflicts, which have left an indelible mark on their societies and culinary traditions. I selected these countries because, much like my beloved Somalia, they have also grappled with ongoing unrest.

Drawing from my own experiences as a refugee and a displaced person, I aim to explore these countries not only to document the obvious, but also to examine the subtle nuances that inherently bind us together. From the simple joys of everyday life to the rituals of setting the dinner table and the connections often forged over a shared meal, I seek to uncover the common threads that unite us all.

When it came to photographers, I traveled to Congo, El Salvador, Lebanon, and Liberia with Riley Dengler, a Brooklyn-based filmmaker and photographer boasting over a decade of experience. Riley and my husband were college buddies, and I've long admired his work. So I knew that journeying to the aforementioned countries with him would not only ease the trip but also provide the comfort one seeks when covering challenging stories or exploring new territories. Riley not only captures stunning images but also possesses an innate ability to put everyone at ease, a quality that shines through in the photos within this book.

Securing images in Afghanistan posed a challenge for me, as I lacked contacts in the country. However, as with much of this book, finding the right person was just a few connections away. My friends at Ziba Foods introduced me to their photographers Omer Khan, Mahab Azizi, and Belal Mostamand. Ziba Foods directly collaborates with small-scale farms and cooperatives, ensuring the sourcing of only the highest quality heirloom and wild-grown dried fruits and nuts from Afghanistan.

For the Egypt chapter, I collaborated with my friend Doaa Elkady, who, though based in Queens, New York, has deep Egyptian roots. She journeyed to Egypt to capture her homeland and its people,

even lending a hand as a model for some of the food shots in the book. Her wonderful energy radiates throughout these pages.

In Iraq, my team at Ten Speed connected me with Aline Deschamps, a French Thai photographer who splits her time between Paris and Lebanon. I had the fortune of meeting her in person in Brooklyn during one of her summer travels. Because she has extensive experience in Iraq, working with various newspapers and projects, capturing photos for the book was relatively easy and safe for her.

In Yemen, I collaborated with Somaya Samawi, whose work captures moments of beauty, resilience, and hope, challenging stereotypes and offering a more nuanced perspective on Yemen and its people. Her work serves as a powerful reminder of the universal humanity that binds us all, transcending borders and barriers. I was fortunate to meet Samawi through my friend Mokhtar Alkhanshali, whom I also interviewed for the Yemen chapter.

In Brooklyn, New York, Julia Gartland assisted in bringing the recipes to life in a rented studio in Bushwick. Those four days of cooking recipes from the book, shooting photos, and laughing together will linger in my memory for quite some time.

For interviews, I chose one or two individuals from each country and the diaspora. I've long believed that to truly understand a place, one must understand its people and its food. I was fortunate to meet many of our subjects in person, while for others, I relied on WhatsApp, Zoom, and voice notes. In *Setting a Place for Us*, you'll meet Mikey, an activist and community organizer in Beirut, Lebanon. You'll be charmed by the passionate and hardworking Emily from Kinshasa, in the Democratic Republic of Congo, whom everyone goes to for beignets. You might see yourself in

Francisco Martinez, a coffee farmer in the highest part of the Cordillera del Bálsamo, the central mountain belt of El Salvador, for whom coffee—growing it, roasting it, drinking and sharing it—is a way of life.

Through their stories and others, you will see how the chaos of human strife impacts the foodways of entire cultures—and ultimately how identity and culture endure through cooking and sitting down to share a meal. These stories and recipes are precious because they are so deeply human and because, through them, people can preserve their heritage. They are about the warmth that we find through coming together to eat a meal no matter our external circumstances.

My life has been shaped by conflict. Its trajectory, its blessings, its many triumphs and sorrows were born out of forces outside of my control. Though my origins begin with war and pain, my story hardly ends there. My hope is that in reading this book, you'll not only learn new recipes but also discover commonalities between your life and the stories recounted here.

A NOTE ON THE RECIPES

I am frequently asked about the pronunciation of recipe names, whether the recipes have been created by me or by others. In this book, I want us to learn together—not only about the places and people but also the correct pronunciation of the delicious recipes featured. To facilitate this, I have included a QR code so you can easily access audio pronunciations of these beautiful recipes. My hope is that you will utilize the code and refer to each recipe by its correct name.

What It Means to Be a Displaced Person

A displaced person is someone who has been forced to leave their home or habitual residence due to a variety of reasons, including conflict, persecution, violence, natural disasters, or human rights violations. Displacement can occur within the borders of the person's own country (internally displaced person, or IDP) or across international borders (refugee).

PANTRY: INGREDIENTS AND EQUIPMENT

I strongly believe that a varied pantry and a few essential ingredients are all you need to effortlessly create a wide range of dishes. In this book, my goal is to demonstrate the art of blending spices, offering straightforward instructions to help you easily follow along and gradually build a remarkable pantry of your own. I understand the limitations of home kitchens, so I've kept the recipes simple and accessible, and thus suitable for cooks of any skill level, and made sure most of the ingredients are readily available, especially if you have a well-stocked spice shop nearby. If you don't, my preferred online sources are Kalustyan's (foodsofnations.com) and Burlap & Barrel (burlapandbarrel.com). I have also ensured you won't need any fancy equipment or hard-to-find gadgets to make these recipes. My equipment recommendations follow the ingredients list.

INGREDIENTS

Achiote. This spice and coloring agent gives the Salvadoran pastelitos on page 124 their distinctive and vibrant orange color. It's used in many cuisines of the world and is known by a variety of names, including annatto, roucou, and achuete, among others. While it is mainly used for coloring, it also imparts an earthy, slightly bitter flavor. Look for it in Central or South American markets or online.

Amaranth. Also known as green amaranth leaves or callaloo, amaranth is a leafy green found in African, Asian, and Caribbean markets and is becoming more widely available at farmers' markets and health food stores because of its amazing health benefits. It's quick to grow, and the young leaves can be eaten raw as a salad and the mature ones can be stewed, as in Bitekuteku | Stewed Amaranth (page 78). The mature greens have a slightly bitter flavor reminiscent of spinach.

Beans and Other Legumes. A common thread running through the chapters of this book, beans and other legumes are pantry and wallet friendly, having long been a smart way to stretch kitchen dollars because they are full of fiber and protein. When cooking dried beans, don't forget the overnight soak. If you're short on time, you can also cover the beans with water in a saucepan, bring the water to a quick, full boil, remove from the heat, and let the beans soak in the hot water for an hour before proceeding with the recipe.

Bouillon/Maggi. These products are convenience foods developed in modern times that have worked their way into traditional dishes in this book. Just a bit of either one (or both) packs a punch of flavor (and salt). They're also inexpensive and shelf-stable, which is why so many home cooks rely on them. Bouillon cubes and granules are easy to find. If you can't find Maggi Seasoning sauce, you can use an equal amount of Worcestershire sauce or

powerhouse. It can be boiled, fried, or stewed and is also dried and ground into flour. The leaves of the plant are edible as well—used in this book in Pondu | Cassava Leaf Stew (page 72).

Chayote. Prized for its subtle, mildly sweet flavor with a hint of nuttiness, chayote is often likened to a cross between a cucumber and a zucchini. It's utilized in cuisines around the world, from Latin America and the Caribbean to Asia and the Mediterranean, and can be eaten raw, pickled, or cooked. In this book, it is used in the Salvadoran recipe for Sopa de Res | Beef Shank Soup (page 127).

Chickpeas. Meaty and nutty in flavor, chickpeas are a great source of plant-based protein. They are a good stand-in for meat and helpful in stretching a bit of meat to feed more people. Canned chickpeas are a great convenience product, but cooking dried chickpeas adds a silkiness to recipes, such as Halabessa | Hot Chickpea Broth/Drink (page 90).

Cilantro. This leafy, deep green herb is grown from coriander seeds, which are a popular spice (see entry for coriander, opposite). The flavor of cilantro can be polarizing, especially for people who carry a genetic trait that makes it taste like soap. It is the most frequently used fresh herb in this book, however, so if you don't like the taste, you can substitute fresh flat-leaf parsley or basil.

Cinnamon. A true workhorse in the kitchen of many countries, cinnamon has a sweet, warm flavor that lends itself to savory dishes, desserts, and beverages. Look at the recipes for Macarona Béchamel | Baked Pasta (page 97), Horchata de Morro | Chilled Rice Drink (page 119), and Arroz con Leche | Rice Pudding (page 136) to see just three of the many ways it can be used.

liquid aminos. If you cannot find Maggi Seasoning cubes, you can use equal amounts chicken bouillon cubes.

Cardamom. Appreciated for its warm flavor with back notes of pepper and citrus, cardamom is sold as pods, seeds, and ground (and all three forms are called for in this book). Cardamom is available in two different botanical genera—green, which has a sweet, citrusy flavor, and black, which is aged and has a deeper, more bitter flavor. Use green cardamom for the recipes in this book.

Cassava. Sometimes labeled yuca, cassava is a dense, starchy root vegetable with a hard, dark brown skin. It must be cooked before it's eaten. It's one of the most popular vegetables in the world because it's easy to grow and is a nutritional

Coriander. Whether used on its own or in a mix, such as Baharat | 7 Spice Mix (page 203), coriander—seeds or ground—adds a tart, almost citrusy note to many of the long-cooking dishes in this book. For the fullest flavor, buy whole seeds, toast them, and then grind them in a spice grinder as needed.

Cumin. Often used in tandem with coriander, think of cumin as coriander's slightly more savory, earthier sibling. It is an essential spice in many parts of the world, from the Middle East to Africa, from Mexico to India. It's in most of the spice blends in this book, and for good reason! As is true with coriander, try to buy cumin seeds rather than ground cumin. Then toast them and grind them just before using for superior flavor.

Dates. Good dates can be eaten on their own as a breakfast, snack, or dessert. They are also used in two recipes in this book, one for cookies (page 170) and one for a pudding-like dish (page 266) that makes a great breakfast or dessert. Dates are the fruits of the date palm tree and are enjoyed fresh or dried, though many people are familiar only with the dried version. (If you get the chance to try fresh ones, don't pass it up. They're delicious!) Soft, sweet Medjool dates are my favorite variety.

Dill, fresh and dried. Like cilantro, dill can be a polarizing flavor. Mint and parsley are good substitutes if you really don't like dill. That said, I encourage you to try it in small amounts, as you just might develop a taste for its sweet, grassy flavor with a hint of anise.

Eggplant. Meaty with a mild, slightly sweet flavor, eggplant is a hearty vegetable that stands up to long cooking and pairs well with meat. It also works well as the star of a vegetarian dish, such as Maghmour | Eggplant and Chickpea Stew (page 193). Look for small to medium eggplants (the larger ones tend to be seedy and are often bitter) that are smooth and shiny and feel heavy for their size.

Fava beans. Both fresh and dried favas are a staple bean in the cooking of the Middle East and Mediterranean. Used in salads, dips, fritters, and stews, they're creamy, taste slightly nutty, and are very filling. Look at Ta'ameya | Fava Bean Fritters (page 92) and Foul Moudammas | Fava Bean Stew (page 252) to see just two of the many ways to use them. The dried version is available unpeeled or peeled and split. The recipes in this book call for peeled dried split favas. If you can find only unpeeled favas, you will need to peel them after you soak them. Canned favas, which can sometimes be used in a pinch, are available at some Middle Eastern and Italian markets.

Fenugreek. An essential ingredient in Saltah | Lamb Stew with Fenugreek Froth (page 255), fenugreek is a frequent addition to the condiments, pickles, and spice mixes enjoyed in many of the countries featured in this book. The dark yellow, squarish seeds are bitter when raw, but once they are cooked, they add a sweet, maple-like flavor to dishes. A little fenugreek goes a long way, so it is typically used sparingly, except in the Yemeni Saltah recipe, where it is the main event.

Ghee. The South Asian term for clarified butter, ghee is made by melting and clarifying regular butter, which is made up of butterfat, milk solids, and water. To clarify butter at home, melt a pound of butter in a medium skillet. After a few minutes, the water will sink to the bottom, and the milk solids (proteins) will rise to the surface. Skim off the milk solids with a spoon and discard, leaving the clear golden liquid—the butterfat—below, which you can pour or ladle off, being careful not to

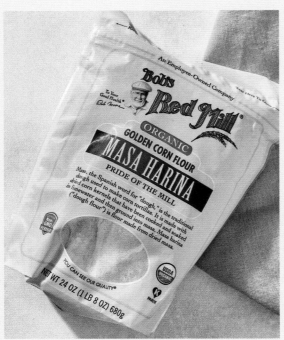

collect any residual water on the bottom. You can buy ghee in glass jars in good supermarkets. It is a great fat for cooking because, with the milk solids removed, it has a higher smoke point than butter.

Ginger, fresh and dried. Both fresh ginger and ground dried ginger make their way into many recipes in this book. Ground dried ginger has a milder flavor than fresh and brings a warmth and brightness to baked goods and spice mixes. Chopped fresh ginger adds a lively spicy-sweet heat to long-cooked dishes like Pondu | Cassava Leaf Stew (page 72) and Moambe | Chicken Peanut Stew (page 73). When buying fresh ginger, look for plump hands that feel heavy for their size and have no wrinkles. Store fresh ginger, well wrapped, in the vegetable drawer of your fridge.

Honey. Honey was first used in prehistoric times, so it's no wonder it appears as a sweetener in traditional dessert recipes in this book. Honeys differ in flavor and color based on the plant from which the bees collected their nectar. A sweet, floral wildflower honey was used for testing the recipes in this book, but you can use any honey you like. The darker the honey, the more pronounced the flavor will be.

Lamb. Lamb and mutton are eaten in many countries featured in this book where meats from other animals such as pork are prohibited for religious reasons. Mutton is older and gamier than lamb and most often used for such long-cooked preparations as Yemeni Saltah | Lamb Stew with Fenugreek Froth (page 255). Younger, milder lamb would be better for something like Kibbeh Nayeh | Raw Kibbeh (page 187). Sheep are economical animals to raise, growing to maturity faster than some other livestock.

Masa. The essential ingredient in Pupusas con Curtido | Filled Masa Flatbreads with Cabbage Slaw (page 131), masa is a dough made from ground corn (masa harina), though it is *not* interchangeable with cornmeal. Both are made from field corn, but the corn for masa is dried and then cooked and soaked in a solution of slaked lime and water—a process called nixtamalization, which gives masa its unique savory flavor. You can find masa harina for making pupusas in larger grocery stores and in Latin and Central American markets. I recommend using the Maseca brand instant corn masa flour.

Mint, dried and fresh. Dried mint appears in a number of recipes in this book—sometimes as a finisher, as in Aush | Vegetable Soup with Noodles and Legumes (page 46), and other times as a primary seasoning ingredient, such as in Malfouf | Cabbage Rolls (page 185). Like fresh mint, dried mint is cooling but has an earthiness that fresh mint doesn't. When you're looking for a fresher, cooling addition, use fresh mint as a last-minute addition to raw dishes, such as Salatet Summaq | Sumac Salad (page 155).

Morro seeds. A primary ingredient in Horchata de Morro | Chilled Rice Drink (page 119), morro seeds have an earthy, molasses-like flavor and resemble flat brown lentils (but are not related to them). They are the seeds of a hard green fruit attached to the morro tree and are dried in the sun before using. They can be difficult to find, but if you are set on making the horchata recipe, you can source morro seeds at Latin and Central American groceries and online.

Nuts (especially almonds, walnuts, and pine nuts). Nuts have long been a staple in the cuisines of the Middle East, in both sweet and savory dishes, such as Sfouf | Semolina Turmeric Cake (page 207) and Mouhamara | Spicy Walnut and Red Pepper Dip (page 204), and in spice mixes, such as Dukkah | Nut and Spice Blend (page 101). They are a great source of monounsaturated fats and antioxidants, so they are useful for maintaining a healthy diet when other foods are scarce. While nuts are not completely interchangeable in texture and flavor, if you don't have one nut on hand for a recipe, you can usually substitute another one with similar results. Many recipes in this book call for toasted nuts. To toast nuts, spread them on a sheet pan, place in a preheated 350°F oven, and toast until they smell nutty and have darkened a shade or two, 5 to 8 minutes, depending on the type of nut.

molasses, sold in bottles in Middle Eastern grocery stores and well-stocked supermarkets, is made by reducing pomegranate juice down to a syrup. It is used two ways in Harak Osbao | Lentils with Crispy Pita and Pomegranate (page 190), to flavor the lentils as they cook and to finish the dish, where it adds a pop of acidity and sweetness and is joined by a small handful of pomegranate seeds, botanically known as arils.

Red palm oil. Palm oil is an edible oil derived from the fruit of the oil palm tree. Red palm oil is the unrefined (less processed, more highly flavored) version of this oil. The refinement process removes fewer nutrients, which makes red palm oil a potentially healthier alternative to standard (and often maligned) palm oil. Palm oil has a distinct flavor profile that can be described as mildly nutty and earthy. Once you open a jar, store it in a cool, dry place for the longest life.

Rice. Whether served as a side or a main dish, rice is in almost every chapter in this book and is a staple for over half of the world's population. I used long-grain white rice for most of the recipes in this book, which is easy to find, shelf-stable, and inexpensive.

Scotch bonnet chile. The chapters in this book on Congo and Liberia will have you headed to the store to source Scotch bonnet chiles. Similar in heat to habaneros, they are very hot!—anywhere from 12 to 140 times hotter than a jalapeño. If you don't regularly handle hot chiles, wear gloves when prepping them for these recipes, but don't skip them. That heat, along with their sweet fruit flavor, will make your food sing.

Smoked fish/salt fish. Dried smoked fish imparts a rich, subtly smoky taste and is a popular flavoring in Congo. Salt fish, preserved through drying and salting, provides a salty intensity and requires long

Peanuts. Native to South America, peanuts, also known as groundnuts, offer a remarkable range of culinary possibilities and are enjoyed in a variety of ways. They can be consumed raw, roasted, boiled, or processed into peanut butter. Roasted peanuts are a favored snack, while peanut butter is a household staple globally. In cooking and baking, peanuts are frequently used to enhance the flavor and texture of dishes, such as stir-fries, curries, salads, and desserts. In this book, you'll find peanuts used in recipes in the Congo and Liberia chapters.

Pomegranate. Cultivated since ancient times, pomegranates are said to have originated in Iran, Afghanistan, and Pakistan. Their tart-sweet flavor can be found in many recipes from those areas, in both sweet and savory dishes. Pomegranate

soaking before use. It is used in a variety of dishes, from soups and stews to fritters, particularly in West African cuisines. Both are prized for their versatility and the depth of flavor they add to a range of recipes, including Fumbwa | Wild Spinach Stew (page 71) and Pondu | Cassava Leaf Stew (page 72).

Sumac. This popular Middle Eastern spice is made from crimson red sumac berries, which are dried and then ground. It has a tangy, citrusy taste and is most often used as a last-minute sprinkle on dishes to preserve its bright flavor. Sumac can be found at well-stocked spice markets, but if you don't have it on hand, a squeeze of lemon juice or a splash of vinegar is a decent substitute.

Tahini/sesame seeds. Sesame seeds and tahini (a butter or paste made from ground hulled sesame seeds) are featured in a number of recipes in this book. The earthy, slightly bitter flavor of tahini adds a creamy, nutty element. When shopping for the seeds or tahini, make sure to buy from a reputable source. Because the seeds are very oily, they can go rancid easily, and that's a flavor you *don't* want to add to your food.

Tomato. Do I really need to write about a tomato? Maybe I do, as tomatoes are featured in every chapter in this book. A perfect fresh ripe tomato—sweet, juicy, and a little acidic—helps create the ideal balance in many recipes. When fresh tomatoes are out of season, substitute high-quality canned tomatoes in sauces and stews. Plum tomatoes are great for cooking because they are meaty with fewer seeds and are reliably available.

Turmeric. A relative of ginger, turmeric is a bright yellow-orange root that you will most often find dried and ground (though fresh turmeric is fun to cook with, too!). Its flavor is a cross between mustard and ginger, and just a small amount will add a gorgeous yellow hue to your dishes. Sfouf | Semolina Turmeric Cake (page 207) and Turshi | Mixed Vegetable Pickles (page 51) are two recipes that owe their sunny color to turmeric.

Yogurt/Labneh. In this book, yogurt adds a creamy tartness to Mantu | Dumplings Stuffed with Lamb/Beef (page 47) and Borani Banjan | Stewed Eggplant with Garlic Yogurt (page 45) and is the base for a refreshing Afghan drink (page 37). Use a plain whole-milk Greek yogurt with as few additives as possible. Whole milk will help prevent sauces from breaking, and the fewer the additives, the more the clean flavor of dairy can shine through. If you can source labneh, which is made the same way as Greek yogurt but with even more of the whey strained off, by all means use it here. It is a bit thicker, richer, and tangier than Greek yogurt.

EQUIPMENT

In this book, the equipment needs have been kept simple for two reasons: respect for the practical-ities of home kitchens and recognition that the rich culinary traditions behind these dishes, not the equipment, are what make the recipes special. You won't need any fancy or hard-to-find utensils or tools. Just stick to your standard kitchen gear:

Two sharp knives (a large one and a paring knife)

A sturdy cutting board for prep work

Bowls for mixing and serving

A colander and a fine-mesh sieve for draining and straining

A stand mixer

A handheld electric mixer

A steamer setup

Wooden spoons

A potato masher

Tongs

A wire skimmer for frying

Metal skewers

Your trusty pots and pans, including a cast-iron skillet, a nonstick pan, a large Dutch oven or other heavy pot with a lid, and small, medium, and large saucepans

When it comes to blending, chopping, and grinding ingredients, use a high-speed blender for purees and other smooth mixtures with plenty of liquid and opt for a food processor when you need a finer chop. An electric coffee grinder works great for grinding spices. If you're without these gadgets, a mortar and pestle will do the trick.

AFGHAI

LEARN HOW TO PRONOUNCE THE RECIPE NAME

IISTAN

AFGHANISTAN

Gardens in Afghanistan, rooted in tradition, stand as a testament to the resilience and cultural richness of the region. Throughout history, they have served as places of contemplation, leisure, and social gatherings, where poets, scholars, and rulers convened to exchange ideas and seek respite from the challenges of their times.

One of the most famous examples is the Babur Gardens in Kabul, originally laid out by the Mughal emperor Babur in the early sixteenth century. They boast expansive lawns, flowing water channels, and vibrant flower beds, providing an escape from urban life.

Another notable Kabul garden is the Bagh-e Bala, a historic park located on the slopes of the Sher Darwaza Mountain. Dating back to the sixteenth century, this garden offers breathtaking views of the city below and serves as a popular recreational spot for locals and tourists alike.

However, decades of conflict and instability have taken a toll on Afghanistan's cultural legacy, including its gardens. Despite the adversity, efforts to restore and preserve these invaluable treasures persist, driven by a collective desire to reclaim Afghanistan's identity and heritage.

BACKGROUND

Afghanistan, covering about 652,230 square kilometers (251,827 square miles), is a vast landlocked country in South Asia, bordered by Iran, Pakistan, Turkmenistan, Uzbekistan, Tajikistan, and China. With a population of around 43 million in 2024, it has a rich history marked by conflict and cultural heritage. Despite its beauty, Afghanistan has faced turmoil, including the Soviet invasion in 1979, the

rise of the Taliban, and ongoing instability, impacting both its people and its heritage.

CIVIL WAR

The civil war in Afghanistan, from 1979 to 1992, began with the Soviet invasion and resistance by the Mujahideen. This conflict saw heavy involvement from foreign powers and massive casualties. The Mujahideen, backed by the United States and other nations, fought against Soviet forces and the Afghan communist government. The war led to the eventual rise of the Taliban, who further destabilized the country. The persistent conflict during and after this period left deep scars on Afghanistan's society and cultural landmarks, including its historic gardens.

2024

Afghanistan today grapples with severe challenges, including persistent violence, weak infrastructure, and high poverty levels. The return of the Taliban in 2021 has further compounded the instability. Despite international aid and efforts to restore cultural sites like the Babur Gardens and Bagh-e Bala, economic growth remains sluggish. Efforts to preserve and reclaim Afghanistan's cultural heritage continue amid ongoing political and security issues, reflecting the nation's enduring struggle to rebuild and maintain its identity.

ALI ZAMAN

Ali Zaman, a New York City coffee-shop owner and native of Queens with a heart deeply rooted in Afghanistan, is a culinary enthusiast with a passion for sharing the flavors of his heritage.

When it comes to Afghan cuisine, Ali's mind drifts to Uzbeki Kabuli pulao (rice and lamb pilaf), the national dish of Afghanistan, with influences from Kabul, his father's hometown, and from Maimana, his mother's birthplace. This flavorful delight becomes irresistible when infused with toasted sesame oil, he says.

Ali shares with me that while Afghanistan often remains overlooked for its natural beauty, he knows its true allure. From the stunning landscapes of Bamyan to the historical charm of Mazar-e-Sharif, each corner holds a piece of history and warmth that captivates.

For Ali, passing down his food traditions is a mission close to his heart. Thanks to his dear friend Hamed, he's delved deep into Afghan culinary treasures. Bonding over cooking childhood favorites during the COVID-19 pandemic, they created memories infused with stories of Afghanistan and New York, a legacy Ali is determined to preserve for future generations.

When I asked Ali where "home" is, he replied, "Home isn't merely a place on the map; it's a feeling that transcends borders." Whether he's in Queens, Afghanistan, or among loved ones in various cities, he proudly states that home is where cherished

memories are made and shared. Reflecting on his journey, Ali takes pride in the friendships he has formed and the restaurant group he has been a part of, each moment shaping him into the person he is today.

In essence, Ali's story is woven together with flavors, experiences, and cherished connections, each thread contributing to the vibrant tapestry of his life.

This creamy, slightly salty drink is a refreshing afternoon pick-me-up on hot summer days. Make sure all of your ingredients are very cold and serve the drink in chilled glasses. Some versions of this recipe call for the addition of seltzer for a little fizz.

DOOGH

Yogurt Drink

MAKES ABOUT 4 CUPS

2 cups plain whole-milk Greek yogurt

1 cup ice-cold water

2 Persian cucumbers, chopped

¼ cup loosely packed fresh mint leaves, plus more for garnish

Juice of ½ lemon

1 teaspoon kosher salt

2 cups ice cubes

In a blender, combine the yogurt, ice water, cucumbers, mint, lemon juice, salt, and ice cubes and blend until very smooth and frothy. Taste and adjust with more salt if needed.

Pour into chilled glasses, garnish with mint, and serve.

In Afghan families, recipes for this crisp, flaky stuffed flatbread are often passed down through the generations. It makes an excellent appetizer or starter for a larger meal and is typically paired with a simple dipping sauce of plain yogurt mixed with a little garlic and olive oil or a chutney, such as the one on page 52. In some households, bolani are a popular choice for afternoon or evening tea gatherings.

BOLANI

Stuffed Flatbread

MAKES 4 FLATBREADS

DOUGH

2 cups all-purpose flour, plus more for the work surface

1 teaspoon kosher salt

2 tablespoons extra-virgin olive oil

½ cup cold water, plus more as needed

FILLING

1 large russet potato, peeled and cut into 1- to 2-inch chunks

Kosher salt

1 cup loosely packed fresh cilantro leaves, chopped

2 green onions, chopped

1 jalapeño chile, seeded, if desired, and finely chopped

1 teaspoon ground coriander

2 tablespoons extra-virgin olive oil

Extra-virgin olive oil for cooking

To make the dough: In a medium bowl, stir together the flour and salt. Drizzle in the oil and stir with a fork just until evenly mixed. Drizzle in the water, a little at a time, stirring and tossing with the fork as you go, just until you have a rough dough that holds together. If the dough seems too dry, add a splash more water and mix until it comes together.

Turn the dough out onto a lightly floured work surface and knead until it forms a soft, smooth ball, about 2 minutes. Wrap with plastic wrap and let rest at room temperature while you make the filling.

To make the filling: In a medium saucepan, combine the potato with salted water to cover and bring to a simmer over medium heat. Cook until the potato is very tender, 15 to 18 minutes.

Drain the potato and transfer to a medium bowl. Using a fork, mash while still hot. Stir in the cilantro, green onions, chile, and coriander, mixing well. Drizzle with the oil, season with 1 teaspoon salt, and mash lightly with the fork to incorporate the oil and salt. Set aside.

Divide the dough into four equal pieces, shape each piece into a ball, and cover the balls with a kitchen towel.

Clean the work surface and then dust again with flour. Remove a ball from under the towel, and using a rolling pin, roll it into a thin 8-inch round, flouring the dough as needed to keep it from sticking. Spoon

one-fourth of the filling over half of the dough round, leaving a ½-inch border along the edge. Fold over the other half to form a half-moon and press the edges together to seal. Flatten gently with your palm to press out any air pockets and to even out the filling. Repeat with the remaining dough balls and filling.

Heat a large cast-iron skillet or griddle over medium-high heat. When it is hot, brush the bottom generously with oil and add as many bolani as will fit without crowding. Cook until the underside is crisp and golden and the dough is no longer raw, 3 to 4 minutes. Flip and cook the second side in the same manner, then transfer to a plate and keep warm. Repeat with the remaining bolani.

Cut the bolani into wedges and serve hot.

Making panir is similar to making ricotta, with the exception that panir is drained longer to ensure a firm ball that is sliceable. It's one of the easiest (and fastest) cheeses you can make, so it's a great introduction to cheese making. This combination of fresh cheese and dried fruit is a typical afternoon snack, often served with cardamom tea. Using the best-quality milk and cream will help the curds separate better and yield more cheese overall.

KISHMISH PANIR

Homemade Soft Cheese with Raisins

MAKES ONE 3- TO 4-INCH BALL; SERVES 4 TO 6

6 cups organic whole milk

¼ cup heavy cream

3 tablespoons freshly squeezed lemon juice or distilled white vinegar

½ teaspoon kosher salt

Raisins for serving

Cut a double thickness of cheesecloth large enough to line a colander. Rinse the cheesecloth with water, wring well, and then line the colander. Set aside.

In a large saucepan, combine the milk and cream over medium heat and bring slowly to a boil, stirring with a wooden spoon so the mixture doesn't scorch. Once it comes to a boil, turn down the heat to low and stir in the lemon juice. Continue to stir gently in one direction just until the milk begins to curdle, about 1 minute, then remove from the heat and let sit for a few minutes while the milk finishes curdling. You'll see the curds gradually separate from the whey. The curds will look like little white clouds, and the whey will be a creamy, murky liquid. Stir in the salt.

Set the colander in the sink and pour the curds and whey into it. Rinse briefly with cold running water to remove the acidic taste from the lemon. Set the colander over a bowl and let the curds drain until the whey is no longer dripping, about 10 minutes.

Gather up the edges of the cheesecloth to form a bundle and then twist them together to shape the curds into a ball. Place the ball, twisted side down, on a large plate. Place another plate on top and set a weight, such as a can of food, on the second plate. Refrigerate the setup until the ball of cheese is firm, about 30 minutes.

Unwrap the cheese, cut into slices or cubes, and arrange on a serving plate. Scatter the raisins around the plate and serve. Wrap any leftover cheese in plastic wrap and refrigerate for up to 2 days.

This tart and refreshing salad is an everyday addition to Afghan tables and goes with just about anything. It can be served as a side dish to accompany kebabs, rice dishes, or other mains, or it can be paired with bread for a light meal.

SALATA

Afghan Salad

SERVES 2 TO 4

4 tomatoes, finely chopped

4 Persian cucumbers, finely chopped

½ red onion, finely chopped

1 small bunch cilantro, coarsely chopped

¼ cup freshly squeezed lemon juice (1 to 2 lemons)

1 teaspoon kosher salt

½ teaspoon dried mint

In a large bowl, combine the tomatoes, cucumbers, onion, cilantro, lemon juice, salt, and mint and toss well. Taste and adjust with more salt if needed.

Serve right away.

This dish of stewed fruits and nuts is traditionally served for Nowruz, or New Year, which falls on the first day of spring, but it can be enjoyed throughout the year. It's traditionally made with seven dried fruits and nuts, representing the seven elements of life, though you can include what you like. Just keep the total cup amount roughly the same. One of the ingredients, senjed, which is also known as Russian olive and silver berry, is the fruit of the oleaster tree and is sweet like a date when dried. Look for it in Middle Eastern stores. You will need to plan ahead when making this dish, as the fruits and nuts must soak in the water for a couple of days before serving.

HAFT MEWA

Fruit and Nut Salad

SERVES 6 TO 8

½ cup raw walnut halves

⅓ cup unsalted pistachios

¼ cup raw blanched almonds

⅓ cup golden raisins

⅓ cup dried cranberries

⅓ cup dried apricots

¼ cup senjed (see headnote)

½ teaspoon rose water

4 cups boiling water

Put the walnuts, pistachios, almonds, raisins, cranberries, apricots, and senjed in a colander and rinse with cold running water. Drain well and transfer to a large heatproof bowl. Add the rose water and boiling water, let cool, then cover and refrigerate for 2 days, stirring several times a day.

After 2 days, the fruit will have absorbed most of the water and any remaining water will have become a syrup in the bottom of the bowl. Serve the fruit and nuts with the syrup ladled over the top. Store any leftovers in a covered container in the refrigerator for up to 2 days.

This richly flavored vegetarian dish layers three flavors—labneh, eggplant, and tomato. It is a beloved dish enjoyed throughout various regions of Afghanistan. While preparation methods and variations may differ among households and regions, this dish is a staple on Afghan dining tables, often served as part of everyday meals. Serve as is as an appetizer or alongside some flatbread.

BORANI BANJAN

Stewed Eggplant with Garlic Yogurt

SERVES 4 TO 6

¼ cup extra-virgin olive oil, plus more as needed

2 medium eggplants (about 1¼ pounds total), cut crosswise into ½-inch-thick slices

Kosher salt

3 garlic cloves, chopped

½ teaspoon sweet paprika

¼ teaspoon ground turmeric

4 canned plum tomatoes, chopped, juices reserved

½ cup water

¼ teaspoon cayenne pepper

1 cup labneh or plain whole-milk Greek yogurt

Dried mint for finishing

In a large skillet, heat the oil over medium heat. While the oil heats, lightly season the eggplant slices on both sides with salt. Line a large plate with paper towels and set it near the stove. When the oil is hot, add as many eggplant slices as will fit without crowding and cook, turning once, until golden on both sides, about 3 minutes per side. Using tongs, transfer the eggplant slices to the towel-lined plate to drain. Repeat with the remaining eggplant, adding more oil to the skillet as needed to keep a thin film on the bottom.

Once all of the eggplant is fried, add two-thirds of the garlic, the paprika, and turmeric to the pan. When the garlic is sizzling, add the tomatoes and their juices, water, cayenne, and 1 teaspoon salt and stir well. Bring to a simmer and cook, stirring occasionally, until the tomatoes begin to break down, about 5 minutes.

Return the eggplant slices to the pan, cover, and cook until the eggplant is tender but still holds its shape, about 10 minutes. Uncover and simmer rapidly for a few minutes to thicken the sauce slightly. Taste and adjust with salt if needed.

Meanwhile, in a small bowl, stir the remaining garlic into the labneh. If the labneh is especially thick, stir in a tablespoon or two of water to thin it out a bit.

To serve, spread half of the labneh mixture in a deep serving platter. Arrange the eggplant slices on the labneh and spoon the tomato sauce over the eggplant. Top with the remaining labneh mixture, finish with a sprinkle of mint, and serve.

This thick, hearty soup warms tables during Afghanistan's bitter-cold winters. If you'd like to add a little freshness, stir in a bunch of spinach or other tender green toward the end of the cooking time.

AUSH

Vegetable Soup with Noodles and Legumes

SERVES 8

2 tablespoons extra-virgin olive oil

1 pound ground lamb or beef

1 small yellow onion, finely chopped

2 garlic cloves, finely chopped

2 teaspoons ground coriander

1 teaspoon ground cumin

1 teaspoon sweet paprika

¼ cup tomato paste

4 cups low-sodium chicken broth

4 cups water

One 15½-ounce can kidney beans, drained and rinsed

One 15½-ounce can chickpeas, drained and rinsed

6 ounces spaghetti, broken into 2- to 3-inch pieces

Kosher salt and freshly ground black pepper

Labneh for serving

Dried mint for finishing

In a large Dutch oven, heat the oil over medium heat. Crumble the meat into the pan and cook, breaking it up with a wooden spoon into small crumbles, until no longer pink, about 5 minutes. Add the onion and garlic and cook, stirring occasionally, until the onion is wilted, about 5 minutes. Add the coriander, cumin, and paprika and stir to mix well. Add the tomato paste to the middle of the pot and let it sizzle undisturbed until it darkens a shade or two, 1 to 2 minutes. Pour in the broth and water, stir, and bring to a simmer.

When the mixture is simmering, add the kidney beans and chickpeas, stir well, and simmer until slightly thickened, 10 to 15 minutes. Add the spaghetti, stir to mix, and cook until al dente, a few minutes shy of the cooking time on the package. Season with salt and pepper.

To serve, spoon a dollop of labneh into each individual soup bowl, then ladle the soup on top of the labneh. Top with more labneh and a sprinkle of mint, then serve.

These savory dumplings are traditionally a labor of love, but your work time is shorter if you use purchased dumpling wrappers, as is done here. Both lamb and beef variations are equally popular. The yogurt sauce is also good with Bolani | Stuffed Flatbread (page 38). I use a tiered bamboo steamer to cook as many dumplings as possible at once, but feel free to use any type of steamer.

MANTU

Dumplings Stuffed with Lamb/Beef

MAKES ABOUT 30 DUMPLINGS

GARLIC TOMATO SAUCE

2 tablespoons extra-virgin olive oil

2 garlic cloves, chopped

One 8-ounce can tomato sauce

¼ cup water

Kosher salt

Red pepper flakes for seasoning

DUMPLINGS

2 tablespoons extra-virgin olive oil, plus more for oiling the steamer

1 pound ground lamb or beef

1 small yellow onion, finely chopped

2 garlic cloves, finely chopped

2 teaspoons ground coriander

2 teaspoons ground cumin

Kosher salt

About 30 store-bought 3-inch square dumpling wrappers, such as wonton wrappers

To make the tomato sauce: In a small saucepan, heat the oil over medium heat. When the oil is hot, add the garlic. When the garlic begins to sizzle, pour in the tomato sauce and water, stir well, and bring to a simmer. Cook, stirring occasionally, until thickened, about 5 minutes. Season with salt and red pepper flakes. Set aside in the pan.

To make the dumplings: In a large skillet, heat the oil over medium heat. Crumble the meat into the pan and cook, breaking it up with a wooden spoon into fine crumbles, until no longer pink, about 5 minutes. Add the onion, garlic, coriander, cumin, and 1 teaspoon salt and cook, stirring occasionally, until the onion is wilted and meat is cooked through, 8 to 10 minutes. Remove from the heat, transfer to a bowl, and let cool. Taste and adjust with more salt if needed.

Place the bowl of cooled filling, a small bowl of cool water, and the dumpling wrappers on your work surface. Keep the wrappers covered with a kitchen towel to prevent drying. Lay a few dumpling wrappers on your work surface. Put a scant tablespoon of filling in the center of each wrapper. Dip your finger into the water and lightly wet the entire edge of each wrapper. Bring two opposite corners together and press to seal. Then bring together the remaining two opposite corners and press to seal, uniting all four corners in the middle. Repeat with the remaining filling and wrappers.

CONTINUED

MANTU

CONTINUED

YOGURT SAUCE

1 cup labneh or plain whole-milk Greek yogurt

1 large garlic clove, finely chopped

Juice of ½ lemon

½ teaspoon dried mint

Kosher salt

Set up a bamboo steamer basket over a pot of simmering water. Brush a little oil on top. Arrange as many dumplings as you can in the basket without their touching. Cover and steam until slightly translucent and tender, about 5 minutes. Set aside in an oven warmer or microwave to keep the cooked dumplings warm. Repeat as many times as needed.

While the dumplings steam, make the yogurt sauce: In a small bowl, stir together the labneh, garlic, lemon juice, and mint, mixing well. Season with salt and set aside.

To serve, reheat the tomato sauce over low heat. Spread about three-fourths of the yogurt sauce on the bottom of a platter (or divide among individual plates). Drizzle with some of the tomato sauce. Arrange the hot dumplings on top of the sauces. If the remaining yogurt sauce is too thick to drizzle, thin with a little water, then drizzle it over the dumplings. Top it with the remaining tomato sauce. Serve right away.

Crisp and refreshing, these pickles are a complementary side to meat or rice dishes or a tasty addition to salads. You can add or subtract vegetables here, based on what you like and what is in season. For example, when small eggplants are in markets, they are often sliced into coins and added to the mix.

TURSHI

Mixed Vegetable Pickles

MAKES 8 CUPS

2 cups distilled white vinegar

2 cups water

3 tablespoons pickling salt

1 tablespoon sugar

1 teaspoon dried dill or mint

1 teaspoon black peppercorns

¼ teaspoon ground turmeric

3 cups cauliflower florets

2 carrots, peeled and thickly sliced on the diagonal

3 celery stalks, thickly sliced on the diagonal

2 small turnips, peeled and cut into about 3 by ¼-inch sticks

1 small red onion, cut into ½-inch wedges

2 garlic cloves, crushed and peeled

2 jalapeño chiles, sliced

In a saucepan large enough to hold all the vegetables, combine the vinegar, water, pickling salt, sugar, dill, peppercorns, and turmeric. Bring to a simmer over medium heat and stir to dissolve the salt and sugar, about 1 minute.

Add the cauliflower, carrots, celery, turnips, onion, garlic, and chiles and bring to a boil. Lower the heat to a simmer and simmer for 1 minute, stirring to mix well. Remove from the heat and transfer to a nonreactive 3-quart crock or other container, making sure the vegetables are covered with the brine. Let cool.

Cover and refrigerate for at least 3 days before serving. The pickles will keep for up to 1 month or so.

Afghans favor tart, tangy sauces and pickles, and this vibrant green, flavorful cilantro-based condiment is part of that tradition. It is particularly popular served alongside kebabs and other rich meat dishes, though it also turns up as an accompaniment to everything from rice dishes to flatbreads.

GREEN CHUTNEY

MAKES ABOUT 2 CUPS

2 bunches cilantro
(4 to 5 cups packed)

¼ cup walnut pieces, toasted

6 garlic cloves, crushed
and peeled

2 small jalapeño chiles, stemmed,
cut into chunks, and some seeds
removed, if desired

2 teaspoons kosher salt

1 cup distilled white vinegar

Cut off and discard the tough bottoms of the cilantro stems (you can use the more tender upper stems) and put the cilantro into a blender or food processor. Add the walnuts, garlic, chiles, and salt and process until a chunky paste forms. With the blender running, drizzle in the vinegar in a steady stream until you have a very smooth, bright green sauce.

Serve right away, or pour into a nonreactive container, lay a piece of plastic wrap over the surface to preserve the bright green color, cover tightly, and refrigerate. The sauce will keep for up to 4 days.

DEMOCRATIC REPUBLIC OF CONGO

LEARN HOW TO PRONOUNCE THE RECIPE NAME

DEMOCRATIC REPUBLIC OF CONGO

JUNE 2022

I kid you not. My arrival in Kinshasa follows some of the most hectic, most chaotic travel antics you could imagine. Think of an ongoing shell game, in stages, with a cast of hustlers finding new ways to make you pay for anything and everything. But the night after our arrival, we have a reprieve when we visit the home of Lena Militisi and her husband, Patrick, for dinner. There is instantly this ease among us—them, their kids, me, and even Riley, the blond, blue-eyed photographer for many of the countries featured in this book. Patrick, an entrepreneur in mining and energy, is Congolese, and Lena is Rwandan. Lena and I look so similar, we have an immediate sisterly bond. The food is inconsequential—she's ordered in. But the comfort that the couple affords me in a new place is worth more than any dish she might have served.

The next day when my fixer comes up short, Lena and her family step in and set me on my course for the rest of my time in Kinshasa. They use their resources to introduce Riley and me to Emily (see page 63). We will continue to stay in touch; Lena and Patrick will invite me and my husband to visit them in Rwanda for Christmas.

They provide the ballast I need in a place of constant hustle and bustle. Because what I will remember most from that trip to Congo is the jarring ebbs and flows of concentrated motion: the number of people in places at once, of cars on the road, of money changing hands. The capacity of the US dollar to move fast is breathtaking.

BACKGROUND

The Democratic Republic of Congo (DRC), also known as DR Congo or Congo-Kinshasa, is located in Central Africa and spans approximately 2.34 million square kilometers (0.9 million square miles). It is bordered by Uganda, Rwanda, Burundi, Tanzania,

Zambia, Angola, the Republic of Congo, South Sudan, and the Central African Republic.

Previously known as Zaire, the DRC was explored by Henry Morton Stanley in the 1870s. The Berlin West Africa Conference (1884–1885) granted Leopold II of Belgium control, creating the Congo Free State, where exploitation and disease led to millions of Congolese deaths. In 1908, Belgium took over, renaming it the Belgian Congo. Independence was achieved on June 30, 1960, with Patrice Lumumba as prime minister and Joseph Kasa-Vubu as president.

Joseph-Désiré Mobutu seized power in 1965, renaming the country Zaire. His rule ended with the First Congo War (1996–1997), leading to Laurent-Désiré Kabila's presidency. His assassination in 2001 saw his son, Joseph Kabila, take over, leading to the Second Congo War (1998–2003), one of the deadliest conflicts since World War II.

In the 2018 election, Félix Tshisekedi succeeded Joseph Kabila as president. The DRC, Africa's second largest country and the eleventh largest globally, has a population of about 109 million, with over 200 ethnic groups and nearly 250 languages. Despite its rich natural resources, the DRC struggles with political instability, corruption, and a history of exploitation.

The DRC has the largest UN peacekeeping mission and hosts over 500,000 refugees, with about 450,000 Congolese refugees in neighboring countries. It also has the largest internally displaced population in Africa.

JUNE 2022: DELAYLA (EMILY) NDELELA

What do you do when you love to cook, your name means prosperity, and you want to build a doughnut empire? Why not launch a beignet or mikate franchise with a twenty-dollar investment? *Beignet* is the French word for doughnut, and French is the official language of the Democratic Republic of Congo. There are also four national languages, of which one is Lingala. *Mikate* is the Lingala word for doughnut.

The pathway to fulfilling the goal of cooking and earning an income from making beignets or mikate was not a straight line for Delayla. Like many Congolese nationals, she spent some time in Belgium, and she went to cooking school there. The wonderful thing about cooking school is that it can stir up your creative juices. Education and many years in the kitchen have given Delayla the ability to create her own recipes and successfully fuse different cooking styles and cultures, leading to delicious meals and the mixing of a myriad of spices.

Back home in Kinshasa, everyone eats beignets. They are made locally by women in markets and on street corners and are served hot with peanut butter or hot pepper sauce. The popularity of beignets sold on the streets has not masked the fact that some people are concerned about the unhygienic conditions in which they are prepared. Delayla was one of those concerned and decided to offer beignets instead of bread as an appetizer in her restaurant, which she opened in 2016. This led to a catering business as well. Government

ministers began ordering mikate for large meetings, and her business took off.

The newfound success was cut short by travel to Belgium in 2017 for medical reasons. Delayla returned to Congo in 2019. Then COVID-19 hit. In 2020, like everywhere around the world, most people in Kinshasa were homebound. So Delayla used this opportunity to deliver mikate to her clients. She captured on video her cooking process and posted it on Facebook. Customers were assured that she was using hygienic practices. The result? Orders came pouring in.

Then, when it came time to name her business, she went from Coin de Mikate to Le Coin D-Emikate, or "doughnut corner," a twist on Delayla's Christian name, Emily. A friend's tweet

about this new venture led to a thousand retweets, and Delayla found herself having to keep up with the orders—and she did. Le Coin D-Emikate was on the way to becoming the Congolese McDonald's. She began getting requests from all over the country, and the momentum was there for a global takeover of the mikate made by Le Coin D-Emikate.

In April 2022, Delayla received a certificate of merit for entrepreneurship, which was presented to her by the First Lady of the Democratic Republic of Congo, Mrs. Denise Nyakeru Tshisekedi. Calls are constant from people in Goma, the capital city of North Kivu Province; Belgium; and other locations expressing interest in opening a franchise.

There is no substitute for demanding work. With a set of self-proclaimed "blessed hands," Delayla can make one thousand doughnuts per day. Everyone wants her recipe, but with a franchise model in the works, that information is a secret. And creativity keeps people interested. Beyond serving the usual topping of hot pepper sauce or peanut butter, Delayla is offering chocolate, vanilla, and other flavors. Selling at festivals and other public spaces keeps the brand strong. Stay tuned for Le Coin D-Emikate in the biggest metropolis near you.

On the streets of Kinshasa, you'll find these skewers made with cubes of either goat or beef. Tell your butcher you're making kebabs and ask what cut would be best (sirloin is a good choice if you're using beef). Whichever cut you choose, make sure it is somewhat lean, with just a bit of fat left around the edges. If there is too much fat, it will melt and drip onto the fire, causing flare-ups. If the meat is too lean, it will be dry when it is cooked. These skewers taste best and most authentic when cooked on a charcoal grill or over an open fire, but a gas grill will also do. Onion chunks have been added to the skewers for flavor here, but you can use bell pepper pieces in their place, or you can skip the vegetable and grill only meat.

KAMUNDELE

Beef/Goat Skewers

SERVES 4 TO 6

2 pounds boneless beef or goat kebab meat, cut into 1-inch pieces

2 tablespoons vegetable oil, plus more for brushing

2 tablespoons tomato paste

1 tablespoon Worcestershire sauce or Maggi Seasoning sauce

2 teaspoons sweet paprika

1 teaspoon granulated garlic

1 teaspoon ground ginger

1 teaspoon kosher salt

1 large red onion, cut into 1-inch chunks

1 lemon, halved

Prepare a fire in an outdoor grill for direct cooking over medium-high heat.

In a large bowl, combine the meat, oil, tomato paste, Worcestershire sauce, paprika, garlic, ginger, and salt. Using your hands, toss well to coat the meat evenly with the seasonings.

Thread the meat pieces onto six metal skewers, alternating with the onion chunks and pushing the pieces close together so each skewer is tightly packed. Brush the loaded skewers with oil.

When the fire is ready, brush the grill grates clean, then rub the grates with oil. Set the skewers directly over the fire and cook, turning as needed, until well charred and browned on all sides, 8 to 10 minutes for medium or until cooked to your liking.

Transfer the skewers to a platter and squeeze the lemon halves over the top. Serve immediately.

This traditional Congolese bread is somewhat neutral in flavor on its own, so it's always served with a flavorful, saucy dish, such as a tomato- or peanut-based stew or a peanut soup. Although the dough takes four days to prepare, the cakes are a staple of the Congolese table. Once prepared, they keep well for several days, as long as they remain wrapped in the banana leaves in which they were cooked. Store them in the fridge and reheat them in a microwave or steamer. At the table, pinch off a piece of chikwanga, and holding it with your fingers, use it to scoop up a bit of stew.

CHIKWANGA

Cassava Flour Cakes

MAKES 6 CAKES; EACH CAKE SERVES 1 TO 2

2 pounds cassava

6 sheets banana leaf, each about 12 by 12 inches, rinsed

Using a paring knife, peel the rough brown skin from the cassava. Halve crosswise, quarter lengthwise, and cut into 2-inch chunks. Put the pieces into a large bowl, add cold water to cover, and loosely place a kitchen towel on top. Let soak for 4 days at room temperature, changing the water after 2 days.

At the end of the 4 days, drain the cassava chunks, transfer them to a colander, and rinse very well under cold running water. Then, using the paring knife, cut out the stringy center core from each piece. Working in batches, transfer the chunks to a mortar and mash with a pestle until you have a very smooth paste (or use a food processor).

Divide the paste into six equal portions. On a work surface, knead and roll each portion into a long cylinder about 6 inches in diameter. Roll up each cylinder in a sheet of banana leaf, fold in the ends, and, using kitchen twine, make ties along the length of the cylinder at 1-inch intervals.

Bring a large pot of water to boil. Using tongs, carefully add the wrapped cassava cylinders to the pot and return the water to a gentle boil. Adjust the heat to maintain a simmer, cover, and cook for 3 hours.

Using tongs, remove the cassava bundles from the pot and let cool slightly. Snip the twine on each bundle, unroll and open the banana leaf, and serve.

Dried smoked catfish adds great depth of flavor to this otherwise simple vegetable stew. It's available online and from some African markets. Wild spinach leaves, known as eru in Cameroon, ukazi in Nigeria, and fumbwa in Congo, are very small green leaves. They are difficult to find fresh in the United States but are sold fresh frozen in African stores and online. If you find fresh fumbwa, be sure to rinse the leaves very well, as they can be gritty. If you can find only fresh frozen, thaw them before using. If you cannot find fumbwa, you can substitute a tender green, such as baby spinach.

FUMBWA

Wild Spinach Stew

SERVES 6 TO 8

2 pieces dried smoked catfish, about 6 to 8 ounces total

1 pound fumbwa (wild spinach leaves)

2 cups chicken broth

2 tomatoes, chopped

1 small yellow onion, chopped

3 green onions, chopped

4 garlic cloves, chopped

Pinch of freshly grated or ground nutmeg

Kosher salt and freshly ground black pepper

½ cup creamy peanut butter

3 tablespoons red palm oil

Rinse the catfish very well under cold running water, then break into roughly 1- to 2-inch pieces and put into a medium bowl. Add hot water to cover and let the fish soak until softened, about 10 minutes. Drain the fish and rinse well again.

In a large pot, combine the fumbwa, broth, tomatoes, onion, garlic, and nutmeg. Remove the bones from the catfish and crumble the fish into the pot. Place the pot over medium heat, bring to a simmer, and simmer for 5 minutes.

Season the mixture with salt and pepper, then stir in the peanut butter and oil. Return the mixture to a gentle simmer, cover, and cook, stirring occasionally, until the greens are tender and the stew has thickened, about 20 minutes.

Uncover and continue to cook down the stew until it is very thick, about 10 minutes more. Then serve.

Some versions of this stew add chunks of beef or chicken or eggplant, but this is the Congolese recipe for pondu at its most basic. Cassava leaves are a common ingredient in Congo but aren't easily found outside of Africa. Look for packages of frozen leaves in African stores or online. This stew is traditionally served with Chikwanga | Cassava Flour Cakes (page 68), plantains, or fufu. Fufu is made by pounding boiled starchy root vegetables like cassava, yams, or plantains into a smooth, dough-like consistency.

PONDU

Cassava Leaf Stew

SERVES 6 TO 8

2 pieces dried smoked catfish, 6 to 8 ounces total

2 pounds frozen cassava leaves, thawed

2 cups chicken broth

½ cup tomato puree or chopped tomatoes

⅓ cup red palm oil

6 green onions or 3 spring onions, finely chopped

1 green bell pepper, finely chopped

2 small eggplants, trimmed and cut into small cubes

3 garlic cloves, chopped

1 tablespoon peeled, chopped fresh ginger

1 Scotch bonnet chile (optional)

Kosher salt

Rinse the catfish very well under cold running water, then break into roughly 1- to 2-inch pieces and put into a medium bowl. Add hot water to cover and let the fish soak until softened, about 10 minutes. Drain the fish and rinse well again.

Rinse the cassava leaves very well under cold running water. Then squeeze out the excess liquid. In a large pot, combine the cassava leaves, broth, tomato puree, oil, green onions, bell pepper, eggplant, garlic, ginger, and chile, and season lightly with salt. Remove the bones from the catfish and crumble the fish into the pot. Place the pot over medium heat, bring to a simmer, and simmer, stirring often, until the greens are completely broken down and the stew is thick, 30 to 40 minutes. If the mixture seems to be drying out toward the end of cooking and the greens are not yet ready, add a little water. Serve hot.

This easy-to-make stew, in which chicken is smothered in a tomatoey peanut sauce, is often called the national dish of Congo. The additions of red palm oil and peanut butter make it especially rich and hearty. Serve with plain white rice, boiled cassava, or fried plantains.

MOAMBE

Chicken Peanut Stew

SERVES 4 TO 6

¼ cup red palm oil

2 pounds bone-in, skin-on chicken drumsticks and thighs

Kosher salt and freshly ground black pepper

1 small yellow onion, chopped

3 garlic cloves, chopped

One 8-ounce can tomato sauce

1 teaspoon sweet paprika

1 chicken bouillon cube

½ teaspoon cayenne pepper

¼ teaspoon freshly grated nutmeg

2 cups water

½ cup creamy peanut butter

In a medium Dutch oven, heat the oil over medium heat. While the oil heats, season the chicken pieces on all sides with salt and black pepper. When the oil is hot, add the chicken pieces, skin side down, and cook until browned on the underside, about 3 minutes. Flip and cook until browned on the second side, 2 to 3 minutes more. Transfer the chicken to a plate.

Add the onion and garlic to the pot and cook, stirring occasionally, until the onion starts to wilt, 4 to 5 minutes. Add the tomato sauce, paprika, bouillon cube, cayenne, nutmeg, and water, stir well, and bring to a simmer. Return the chicken to the pot, cover with the lid ajar, and simmer until the chicken is very tender and the sauce is slightly thickened, 35 to 40 minutes.

Put the peanut butter into a small, heatproof bowl, add about 1 cup of the sauce from the pot, and whisk until smooth. Whisk the peanut butter mixture into the simmering sauce in the pot, mixing well. Return the sauce to a simmer and cook, stirring often, just until thick and smooth, about 5 minutes. Serve immediately.

Nearly every home cook in Congo seasons this popular bean dish slightly differently. Some use palm oil, others add some ginger or additional spices or a chile, and still others add a small piece of smoked meat or fish for more flavor. This recipe will point you in the right direction. It is most often served as a main accompanied with plain white rice and fried plantains, but it could also be served as a side to meats.

MADESU

Stewed Red Beans

SERVES 6 TO 8

1 pound dried red or white beans

3 bay leaves

2 yellow onions, 1 halved, 1 chopped

⅓ cup olive oil or vegetable oil

6 green onions or 3 spring onions, chopped

1 small green bell pepper, chopped

5 garlic cloves, chopped

2 cups chopped canned tomatoes, with their juices

2 tablespoons tomato paste

2 chicken bouillon cubes

2 teaspoons sweet paprika

½ teaspoon freshly grated nutmeg

Kosher salt and freshly ground black pepper

Pick over the beans, discarding any grit or misshapen beans. In a large bowl, combine the beans with water to cover by several inches and soak overnight in the refrigerator.

The next day, drain the beans and rinse well. Transfer to a large Dutch oven and add the bay leaves, onion halves, and water to cover by about 1 inch. Place over medium-high heat, bring to a simmer, and cook until the beans are tender and the mixture has thickened, 30 to 40 minutes or so. The timing will depend on the age of the beans.

While the beans are cooking, in a large skillet, heat the oil over medium heat. Add the chopped onion and cook, stirring occasionally, until wilted, about 5 minutes. Add the green onions, bell pepper, and garlic and cook, stirring once or twice, until sizzling and fragrant, about 1 minute more. Stir in the chopped tomatoes and tomato paste and cook, stirring occasionally, until thickened, about 10 minutes. Add the bouillon cubes, paprika, and nutmeg and stir just until the cubes have melted into the mixture. Then simmer, stirring occasionally, until the mixture is thick and dark red, about 5 minutes more. Season with salt and pepper and remove from the heat.

Add the tomato mixture to the beans and bring to a simmer over medium-low heat. Cook, stirring occasionally, until the mixture is thick and creamy and the beans are very tender, 30 to 40 minutes more.

Taste and adjust with salt if needed. Remove and discard the bay leaves and onion halves, then serve.

Salt cod in Congo is not always as heavily salted as salt fish is in other cuisines, so depending on what type of grocery store—Greek, Portuguese, Caribbean, West African, or another—you find your salt cod in, you might have to soak it anywhere from overnight to up to 3 days. To soak it, put it in a bowl with lots of cold water and refrigerate, changing the water every 12 hours. To test if it has soaked long enough, slice off a small sliver, boil it in a little water for a minute or two, and taste. If it's too salty, soak it for another 12 hours.

MAKAYABU

Stewed Salt Fish

SERVES 6

2 pounds skin-on salt cod fillet, cut into 2-inch chunks, soaked (see headnote)

3 tablespoons olive oil or vegetable oil, plus more as needed

1 yellow onion, sliced

2 red or yellow bell peppers, sliced

1 tablespoon tomato paste

3 garlic cloves, chopped

1 tablespoon peeled, chopped fresh ginger

¼ teaspoon cayenne pepper

1 cup chopped canned tomatoes, with their juices

1 cup water

Kosher salt

Drain the soaked fish and pat dry. In a large nonstick skillet, heat the oil over medium-high heat. When the oil is hot, add the fish, skin side down, and cook until crisp and golden on the underside, about 4 minutes. Flip and cook until browned on the second side, about 3 minutes more. Transfer the fish to a plate.

A film of oil should be coating the bottom of the pan. Add a little more oil if needed. Lower the heat to medium, add the onion and bell peppers, and cook, stirring often, until wilted, 3 to 4 minutes. Add the tomato paste, garlic, ginger, and cayenne and cook undisturbed until sizzling and fragrant, about 1 minute. Add the chopped tomatoes and their juices and the water, bring to a simmer, and cook, stirring occasionally, until slightly thickened, 5 to 10 minutes.

Return the fish to the pan and cook, stirring occasionally, until the fish flakes when pressed with a fork, 5 to 10 minutes more. Taste for salt and add if needed (the fish may have provided enough). Serve immediately.

Bitekuteku, also known as green amaranth or callaloo, can be found in African and Asian markets. It is also increasingly available at farmers' markets and at health food stores because it is high in antioxidants, protein, minerals, and vitamins and may reduce inflammation and cholesterol levels. The addition of baking soda to the cooking water helps set the color in the greens. Dried smoked catfish is often added to this dish. If you want to include it, follow the directions in the recipe for Pondu | Cassava Leaf Stew (page 72). Serve hot.

BITEKUTEKU

Stewed Amaranth

SERVES 4 TO 6

2 teaspoons baking soda

1 pound green amaranth leaves, tough stems trimmed

¼ cup red palm oil

6 green onions or 3 spring onions, chopped

1 medium eggplant (about 8 ounces), peeled and cut into 1-inch cubes

1 green or red bell pepper, chopped

1 Scotch bonnet chile (optional)

2 garlic cloves, chopped

1 chicken bouillon cube

1 cup water

Kosher salt

Bring a large pot filled with water to a boil over high heat and add the baking soda. Add the amaranth and cook until wilted, about 5 minutes. Drain into a colander and rinse well under cold running water.

In a large skillet, heat the oil over medium heat. When the oil is hot, add the green onions, eggplant, and bell pepper and cook, stirring and tossing occasionally, until the eggplant begins to wilt, about 8 minutes. Add the amaranth, chile, garlic, and bouillon cube, and then pour in the water. Bring to a simmer and cook, stirring occasionally, until all of the vegetables are very tender and the mixture is thick, 5 to 10 minutes. Season with salt if needed.

Serve hot. Store any leftovers in an airtight container in the refrigerator for 2 to 3 days.

This fiery hot sauce is made with Scotch bonnet chiles, so a little goes a long way. You could stir a splash or two into just about any dish in this chapter to intensify the flavors. Once you have made a batch, it will keep in a tightly capped glass jar in the refrigerator for several weeks.

PILI PILI

Hot Chile Sauce

MAKES SCANT 1 CUP

6 Scotch bonnet chiles

6 red jalapeño chiles

Juice of 1 lemon

3 garlic cloves

1-inch piece fresh ginger, peeled and sliced

1 teaspoon kosher salt

3 to 4 tablespoons water

2 tablespoons neutral oil (such as vegetable or canola)

Wearing gloves, remove the stems from the Scotch bonnets and jalapeños and then remove the seeds, if desired. (The sauce will be much hotter if you leave the seeds in.)

In a blender, combine all of the chiles, the lemon juice, garlic, ginger, salt, and 3 tablespoons of the water and blend to make a thick paste, adding the remaining 1 tablespoon water if needed to move the blades. Add the oil and blend until you have a smooth sauce.

Transfer the sauce to a tightly capped glass jar or other nonreactive container and refrigerate until ready to use.

EGYPT

LEARN HOW TO PRONOUNCE THE RECIPE NAME

EGYPT

In this chapter, Doaa, a photographer based in New York, traveled across Egypt from land to sea, from markets to mosques, to capture the beauty and multilayered identity of this stunning country.

BACKGROUND

Egypt, officially known as the Arab Republic of Egypt, is a transcontinental country that stretches from northern Africa to southwestern Asia. It is bordered by the Mediterranean Sea to the north, Sudan to the south, Libya to the west, and Israel and the Gaza Strip to the northeast, and has a population of about 104 million people, making it one of the most populous countries in Africa and the Arab world. Egypt spans approximately 1,001,450 square kilometers (386,662 square miles).

Its rich historical heritage dates back thousands of years, making it one of the earliest cradles of civilization, with ancient Egypt being known for its pharaohs, pyramids, and other iconic landmarks, such as the Great Sphinx and the Nile River. Throughout its history, Egypt has seen the rise and fall of various dynasties, invasions by foreign powers, and periods of cultural and intellectual flourishing.

In 1952, Egypt gained independence from British colonial rule, marking the beginning of a new chapter in its history. Since then, the country has faced many challenges, including political transitions, social and economic reforms, and regional conflicts. However, it has made significant strides in a variety of sectors, among them infrastructure development, tourism, and agriculture.

Egypt is known for its cultural contributions to the world, including great works of literature and art and a long-standing film industry. It is also a major player in regional politics and a center for Arab media and entertainment.

2024

Throughout its history, Egypt has experienced periods of both political stability and political unrest. It has faced enormous challenges related to governance, economic development, and social inequality. However, it has also made progress in areas such as education, health care, and infrastructure.

RANA ABDELHAMID

Rana Abdelhamid, a passionate advocate and visionary, hails from the vibrant immigrant community of Little Egypt, in Queens, New York. She is the founder and executive director of Malikah, an organization dedicated to empowering women and girls through self-defense training, healing practices, community organizing, and financial-literacy education.

Home for Rana is a blend of Queens, where she was nurtured, and Alexandria, Egypt, her family's ancestral home. These places hold great significance for her, shaping her identity and values. Witnessing her elders' commitment to serving working-class and immigrant communities inspired Rana to dedicate her life to uplifting others as well.

Rana's life in Queens reflects the cultural fusion characteristic of immigrant experiences in New York City. Her father's enterprise in opening the first halal butcher shop in Queens illustrates her family's contribution to making cultural practices accessible.

When I asked Rana what dish best represents her country, Egypt, she replied, "It is chicken over rice." She continued, "This dish is not only delicious but also symbolic of the Egyptian working-class street-vending community in New York City. It's a blend of both New York and Egyptian culinary traditions, reflecting the diverse and dynamic nature of Egyptian culture."

I then asked her what is most misunderstood about Egypt. She replied, "I think one of the most misunderstood things . . . is its people's resilience and creativity in the face of challenges. Egyptian culture is known for its music, art, and cinema. Much of this comes through cultures of resistance and the realities of working-class tradition. I also think that most people don't recognize this."

Amid her many achievements, Rana's fondest memories revolve around gatherings with loved ones that are marked by the aroma of koshary, a nationally cherished Egyptian dish—a flavorful combination of rice, lentils, and macaroni, topped with a spicy tomato sauce, crispy fried onions, and a tangy garlic vinegar sauce—that her mother prepares. These moments evoke a sense of belonging and unity, she says. Talk about walking the walk.

This recipe, also known as hummus al shaam, lands somewhere between a soup and a drink and is especially comforting on a cold day. It is not only a beloved dish but also a symbol of hospitality in many Middle Eastern and North African cultures, where it is often offered to guests as a gesture of warmth and welcome.

HALABESSA

Hot Chickpea Broth/Drink

SERVES 8 TO 10

1 pound dried chickpeas

4 quarts water

2 bay leaves

4 plum tomatoes,
cut into chunks

1 small yellow onion,
cut into chunks

4 garlic cloves, crushed
and peeled

2 tablespoons tomato paste

2 teaspoons ground cumin

Pinch of red pepper flakes

Kosher salt

Juice of 2 lemons, plus
lemon wedges for serving

Pick over the chickpeas, discarding any grit or misshapen beans. In a large bowl, combine the chickpeas with water to cover by several inches and soak overnight in the refrigerator.

The next day, drain the chickpeas and rinse well. Transfer to a Dutch oven and add the water and bay leaves. Place over medium heat, bring to a simmer, and cook for 20 minutes.

Meanwhile, in a blender, combine the plum tomatoes, onion, garlic, tomato paste, cumin, and pepper flakes and blend until smooth.

When the chickpeas have simmered for 20 minutes, stir in the tomato mixture, return the broth to a simmer, and skim off and discard any scum that rises to the surface. Continue to simmer, stirring occasionally, until the chickpeas are almost tender, 40 minutes to 1 hour.

Season with salt (start with 2 teaspoons, taste, and add more if needed), then continue to simmer until the chickpeas are very tender and the broth is flavorful, 15 to 20 minutes more. Stir in the lemon juice.

Ladle the chickpeas and broth into mugs and serve with lemon wedges on the side.

Similar to falafel, these Egyptian fritters are made with dried split favas and rolled in sesame seeds before frying. Serve them as you would falafel: in a pita, on top of a salad, or as a snack on their own with a tahini or other dip. The baking soda helps keep the mixture light.

TA'AMEYA

Fava Bean Fritters

SERVES 4 TO 6

2 cups dried split fava beans

1 small yellow onion, coarsely chopped

1 cup loosely packed fresh flat-leaf parsley leaves

1 cup loosely packed fresh cilantro leaves

3 garlic cloves, crushed and peeled

1 teaspoon ground coriander

1 teaspoon ground cumin

½ teaspoon baking soda

Kosher salt

Vegetable oil for frying

½ cup sesame seeds

Pick over the fava beans, discarding any grit or misshapen beans. In a large bowl, combine the favas with water to cover by several inches and soak overnight in the refrigerator. (Unlike dried whole favas, there is no need to peel split favas, as they are sold already peeled.)

The next day, drain the favas and rinse well. Transfer to a food processor and add the onion, parsley, cilantro, garlic, coriander, cumin, baking soda, and 2 teaspoons salt. Process until a smooth, thick paste forms. Transfer to a medium bowl, cover, and refrigerate until firm, about 1 hour.

Pour oil to a depth of about 2 inches into a Dutch oven and heat to 365°F. Line a large plate with paper towels and set it near the stove.

While the oil heats, spread the sesame seeds on a small plate. Line a sheet pan with parchment paper. Scoop out walnut-size balls of the fava mixture and form each ball into a patty about 1 inch thick. Coat the patties on both sides in the sesame seeds and then set aside on the prepared sheet pan.

Once all of the patties are formed and coated, working in batches to avoid crowding, add the patties to the hot oil and fry until crisp, golden brown, and cooked through, 4 to 6 minutes per batch. Using tongs or a wire skimmer, transfer the fritters to the towel-lined plate and immediately season with salt. Repeat until all the fritters are cooked, always allowing the oil to return to 365°F between batches. Serve the fritters hot.

The filling of this main dish is delicious with bell peppers but will work with zucchini, cabbage leaves, grape leaves, or small eggplant as well. To make a vegetarian version, omit the meat and add an additional ½ cup rice.

FIL FIL MAHSHI

Stuffed Peppers

SERVES 6

½ cup chopped fresh flat-leaf parsley leaves (reserve the stems)

2 tablespoons chopped fresh dill or mint leaves (reserve the stems)

6 bell peppers (any color you like), tops removed and reserved, seeds discarded

6 tablespoons olive oil

12 ounces ground beef or lamb

1 small yellow onion, finely chopped

2 plum tomatoes, seeded and chopped

4 garlic cloves, chopped

2 teaspoons ground coriander

2 teaspoons ground cumin

Kosher salt and freshly ground black pepper

1 cup long-grain white rice

⅓ cup tomato paste

4 cups low-sodium chicken or vegetable broth

Gather the parsley and dill stems into a bundle, tie together with kitchen twine, and set aside.

Select a Dutch oven large enough to hold all of the bell peppers standing and fitting snugly. Place over medium heat and add 2 tablespoons of the oil. When the oil is hot, crumble the meat into the pot, add the onion, and cook, breaking the meat up with a wooden spoon into small crumbles, until the meat is no longer pink, 4 to 5 minutes. Add the chopped tomatoes, chopped parsley and dill, half of the garlic, and the coriander and cumin and season with 2 teaspoons salt and several grinds of pepper. Cook, stirring, until well mixed, 1 to 2 minutes. Stir in the rice, remove from the heat, and let cool just until warm. Stuff the meat-rice mixture into the bell peppers, filling each pepper about three-fourths full to leave room for the rice to expand during cooking. Wipe the Dutch oven clean with a paper towel. Return the Dutch oven to medium heat and add the remaining 4 tablespoons oil. When the oil is hot, add the tomato paste and the remaining garlic and let sizzle, stirring occasionally, for 1 minute. Pour in the broth, then add water as needed so the liquid will reach about halfway up the sides of the peppers (about 1 cup) once the peppers are added. Add the reserved herb stem bundle, then nestle the peppers in the pot and cover them with their reserved tops. Cover the pot and simmer until the peppers are tender and the rice is cooked, 45 minutes to 1 hour.

Carefully transfer the peppers to a serving platter. Remove and discard the herb stem bundle, then taste the sauce, season with salt if needed, and bring to a simmer to reduce slightly, 2 to 3 minutes. Serve the peppers with the sauce spooned over the top.

Similar to a frittata, this quick breakfast or lunch dish is very versatile. Zucchini or greens can replace the bell pepper and cilantro, or a cilantro-mint combo can be used in place of the parsley. Heartier versions sometimes include sautéed ground beef or lamb.

EGGAH

Baked Omelet

SERVES 2 TO 3

2 tablespoons extra-virgin olive oil

½ yellow onion, finely chopped

½ green or red bell pepper, finely chopped

6 large eggs

Kosher salt and freshly ground black pepper

½ teaspoon ground coriander

2 small plum tomatoes, chopped

½ cup finely chopped fresh flat-leaf parsley

Preheat the oven to 375°F.

In a large nonstick skillet, heat the oil over medium heat. When the oil is hot, add the onion and bell pepper and cook, stirring occasionally, until tender, 6 to 7 minutes.

Meanwhile, in a medium bowl, whisk the eggs until blended. Season with 1½ teaspoons salt, several grinds of pepper, and the coriander and whisk to mix.

When the vegetables are ready, pour the eggs into the skillet and sprinkle the tomatoes and parsley evenly over the top. Cook for a minute or two until the edges begin to set, then transfer to the oven and bake until the eggs are set and the top is golden, 10 to 12 minutes.

Using a rubber spatula, loosen the edges of the omelet from the pan, then slide out the omelet onto a serving plate and cut into wedges. Serve warm or at room temperature.

This baked dish, which recalls both Greek pastitsio and Italian pasta al forno, is classic Egyptian comfort food and is often served for large family gatherings and holidays. While there are different methods for building the casserole, the creamiest result comes from mixing the pasta with the white sauce and sandwiching the meat sauce between two layers of silky, rich pasta.

MACARONA BÉCHAMEL

Baked Pasta

SERVES 8

Unsalted butter for the baking dish

Kosher salt for the pasta water

MEAT SAUCE

2 tablespoons extra-virgin olive oil

1 pound ground beef or lamb

1 small onion, finely chopped

2 teaspoons chopped fresh thyme

Two 8-ounce cans tomato sauce

1 cup water

¼ teaspoon ground cinnamon

Kosher salt and freshly ground black pepper

¼ cup chopped fresh flat-leaf parsley leaves

Preheat the oven to 400°F. Butter a 9 by 13-inch baking dish. Bring a large pot of salted water to a boil for the pasta.

To make the meat sauce: In a large skillet, heat the oil over medium heat. When the oil is hot, add the meat, onion, and thyme and cook, breaking the meat up with a wooden spoon into small crumbles, until the meat is no longer pink, about 5 minutes. Add the tomato sauce, water, cinnamon, 1 teaspoon salt, several grinds of pepper, and parsley and stir to mix well. Bring to a simmer and cook, stirring occasionally, until thick and flavorful, about 15 minutes.

CONTINUED

MACARONA BÉCHAMEL

CONTINUED

BÉCHAMEL SAUCE

4 tablespoons unsalted butter

¼ cup all-purpose flour

4 cups whole milk

¼ teaspoon freshly grated nutmeg

Kosher salt

1 large egg

1½ cups shredded low-moisture mozzarella cheese

1 pound tubular dried pasta (such as penne, ziti, or rigatoni)

While the meat sauce cooks, make the béchamel sauce: In a medium saucepan, melt the butter over medium-low heat. When the butter has melted, add the flour, stir until smooth, and continue to cook, stirring constantly, until the mixture smells lightly toasted but does not change color, 1 to 2 minutes. Slowly add the milk while whisking constantly to ensure the mixture is smooth. Whisk in the nutmeg and 1 teaspoon salt, then continue to simmer, whisking occasionally, until thickened, 8 to 10 minutes. Remove the sauce from the heat. Break the egg into a medium bowl, slowly whisk about 1 cup of the hot béchamel sauce into the egg to temper it, and then whisk the mixture back into the sauce. Add half of the mozzarella to the béchamel and stir until melted and smooth.

Add the pasta to the boiling water, stir well, and cook until about 1 minute shy of al dente, according to the package directions. Drain the pasta into a colander and then return it to the pot. Add the béchamel sauce and stir to coat evenly.

To assemble, spread half of the dressed pasta in the prepared baking dish. Spread the meat sauce evenly over the top. Spread the remaining pasta over the meat layer. Sprinkle the remaining cheese over the top. Place the baking dish on a sheet pan to catch any drips and bake until the top is browned and bubbly, 30 to 40 minutes. Let rest for 10 to 15 minutes before serving.

A popular street food in Egypt, these warm sandwiches are filled with quickly cooked cubed beef liver seasoned with warm spices and topped with a squeeze of lemon juice to soften its flavor. The easiest way to cube the liver is to freeze it for 20 to 30 minutes to firm it up before cutting. If you want to gild the lily, add a drizzle of tahini sauce to each sandwich before serving. To make the sauce, in a small bowl, stir together ½ cup tahini and 2 tablespoons freshly squeezed lemon juice, thin with warm water until you get the consistency you want, and season with salt.

KEBDA ESKANDARANI

Beef Liver Sandwiches

SERVES 4

1 pound beef or calf liver, cut into ½- to 1-inch cubes

3 garlic cloves, chopped

1 teaspoon dried mint

1 teaspoon ground coriander

1 teaspoon ground cumin

Kosher salt and freshly ground black pepper

2 tablespoons extra-virgin olive oil

1 small yellow onion, chopped

1 small green bell pepper, chopped

½ cup water

4 crusty sandwich rolls, or 5- to 6-inch baguette pieces, split

Lemon wedges for serving

In a large bowl, combine the liver, garlic, mint, coriander, cumin, 1 teaspoon salt, and several grinds of pepper. Toss to coat the liver evenly with the seasonings and let marinate for 30 minutes.

When the liver has finished marinating, in a large skillet, heat the oil over medium heat. Add the onion and bell pepper and cook, stirring occasionally, until softened, 6 to 7 minutes. Add the liver and cook until browned on the outside, 4 to 5 minutes. Add the water, bring to a simmer, and simmer until the water evaporates and the liver is cooked through, 4 to 5 minutes more. Taste and adjust the seasoning with salt and pepper if needed.

Pile the liver mixture onto the rolls, dividing it evenly, and serve right away, with the lemon wedges on the side.

Dukkah is more than just a spice blend. This traditional spice blend delivers more than just flavor and aroma. It also adds crunch to dishes. It's used as a finisher for meat, seafood, vegetables, eggs, dips—just about anything you can think of. Because there are natural oils in the nuts and seeds that can turn the blend rancid at room temperature, be sure to store it in the refrigerator, where it will keep for about a month.

DUKKAH

Nut and Spice Blend

MAKES SCANT 1 CUP

½ cup chopped blanched almonds or hazelnuts (or a combination)

3 tablespoons sesame seeds

1 tablespoon coriander seeds

1 tablespoon cumin seeds

1 tablespoon fennel seeds

2 teaspoons kosher salt

Put the nuts into a small skillet, set over low heat, and heat, stirring and tossing almost constantly, until lightly toasted, 3 to 4 minutes. Transfer to a small bowl and let cool.

Return the pan to low heat, add the sesame, coriander, cumin, and fennel seeds, and heat, stirring often, until the sesame seeds are lightly golden and all of the spices are fragrant, about 2 minutes. Transfer to the bowl with the nuts and let cool.

Transfer the cooled nuts and seeds to a spice grinder (in batches, if needed) and pulse until crumbly but still coarse. Transfer to a storage container and stir in the salt. Cap tightly and store in the refrigerator.

This eggless version of bread pudding is extra luscious because it's made with pastry instead of bread. You could use baked puff pastry or filo dough here, but croissants make this recipe especially easy. Some recipes call for crumbled palmiers, but that could get a bit expensive, though the result would be equally delicious.

OM ALI

Bread Pudding

SERVES 6

6 day-old good-quality croissants

3 cups half-and-half

½ cup sugar

1 cup cold heavy cream

Dash of pure vanilla extract

¼ cup chopped unsalted pistachios

¼ cup unsweetened dried coconut flakes

¼ cup golden raisins

Preheat the oven to 350°F.

Tear the croissants into bite-size pieces and spread in a single layer on a sheet pan. Bake until crisp, 8 to 10 minutes.

While the croissants are baking, in a medium saucepan, combine the half-and-half and sugar, place over low heat, and bring just to a simmer, stirring to dissolve the sugar. Remove from the heat. In a medium bowl, whisk the cream until soft peaks form, then whisk in the vanilla.

When the croissant pieces are ready, remove from the oven and leave the oven on. Transfer the croissant pieces to a 9 by 13-inch broiler-proof baking dish, spreading them in an even layer. Sprinkle the pistachios, coconut, and raisins evenly over the top. Pour the hot half-and-half mixture over all and let sit for a few minutes so it soaks into the croissants.

Spread the whipped cream over the top, then transfer the dish to the middle rack of the oven and bake until bubbly, about 25 minutes.

Turn on the broiler. With the pudding still on the middle rack of the oven, broil until browned on top, about 3 minutes, depending on the strength of your broiler. Serve warm.

Versions of these butter cookies are found all over the Middle East and are flavored with various extracts, such as orange flower water or rose water. But the Egyptian recipe often calls for just three ingredients: ghee, sugar, and flour. I added a bit of salt to help heighten the other flavors. The nuts on top are optional but add a nice crunch.

GHORAYEBA

Shortbread Cookies

MAKES ABOUT 36 COOKIES

1 cup ghee, at room temperature (not liquid but scoopable for measuring)

¾ cup confectioners' sugar, plus more for dusting (optional)

2 cups all-purpose flour

¼ teaspoon fine sea salt

Unsalted whole pistachios or whole blanched almonds, for topping (optional)

In a stand mixer fitted with the paddle attachment, beat together the ghee and sugar on high speed until very smooth, 1 to 2 minutes. On low speed, add the flour and salt and beat until blended. (Brands of ghee can vary in their water content, so if the dough is crumbly at this point, drizzle in a tablespoon or so of water to bring it together.) Then increase the speed to high and beat until the dough is very creamy and smooth (almost like hummus), 3 to 4 minutes. Cover and refrigerate just until firm, about 1 hour.

Preheat the oven to 325°F. Line two sheet pans with parchment paper.

Scoop up spoonfuls of the dough and roll between your palms into balls 1 inch in diameter. As the balls are shaped, set them on the prepared sheet pans, spacing them about 2 inches apart. Lightly press your thumb in the top of each ball to make a small depression and add a nut to each one, if desired.

Bake the cookies until they are just set to the touch and light golden on the bottom, 12 to 15 minutes. Transfer to a wire rack and let cool completely.

Dust the cooled cookies with confectioners' sugar, if desired. They will keep in an airtight container at room temperature for up to 4 days.

EL SALV

LEARN HOW TO PRONOUNCE THE RECIPE NAME

ADOR

EL SALVADOR

When I initially began to think about this book, the first place I set out for was El Salvador. It is the country in which the blueprint for this project was created. When I got there, I was told a story that had not been shared with me before. I was met with warmth, good food, and inclusion at every café and restaurant and even among the surfers at the beach. This was in direct conflict with what I had been told about the country. I think back to the dangers of single-origin stories. Who gets to shape your stories? And why are ones like El Salvador peppered with words like *dangerous, gangsters,* and *violence*?

Having made many friends in El Salvador in 2020, I returned in 2022 to start the book. I zigzagged from coffee farms on mountaintops to cooking with women on the side of the road to witnessing a new phase of political changes being developed. The country had just undergone significant political shifts, including changes in leadership and reforms in governance structures. It seemed like it was getting a fresh start; new developments were going up, and hope was permeating the air. I am eternally grateful for having learned about El Salvador in a truly intimate way that has allowed me to know a more nuanced story.

BACKGROUND

El Salvador is a small, beautiful country in Central America, covering about 21,041 square kilometers (8,124 square miles). It is bordered by the Pacific Ocean, Guatemala, and Honduras. With fewer than 7 million people, El Salvador has rich soil that is nourished by over twenty volcanoes. Colonized by the Spanish in the sixteenth century, the land was exploited for cash crops and labor, including Indigenous people and enslaved Africans. El Salvador gained independence in the early nineteenth century and banned slavery in 1825, but inequality persisted. By the twentieth century, politics and economics were dominated by a small elite, and the country faced destabilizing economic cycles. Revolutionary peasant movements emerged, influenced by Marxist ideas. In October 1979, a far-right junta's coup led to civil war.

CIVIL WAR

The seeds of the civil war in El Salvador, lasting from 1979 to 1992, were sown by the Spanish-established plantation economy in the sixteenth century and were exacerbated each time agrarian reform was denied. The failure to redistribute land and shift farming to domestic consumption contributed to the war. Peasants, factory workers, students, and others demanded changes. Liberation theology, embraced by Salvadorans, faced hostility

from the Catholic church and Washington. After the October 1979 coup, the army was unleashed on the population, targeting rural workers and committing atrocities, with over 75,000 civilians killed. The conflict, funded by American taxpayers in the name of anti-communism, drew international scrutiny. By 1992, the Soviet Union's collapse led to a United Nations–brokered peace deal, ending the war. About 20 percent of the population had fled, leaving those who stayed with a deeply uncertain future.

CIVIL WAR (1980–1992)

The Church became increasingly involved in social issues, especially during the civil war, when it often took a stand for human rights. Many clergy members, including Archbishop Óscar Romero, advocated for the poor and criticized government abuses. Romero was assassinated in 1980, becoming a martyr and symbol of the Church's commitment to social justice.

2024

El Salvador faces major challenges, including weak infrastructure, high violence, and severe poverty. The country also deals with frequent earthquakes and has high crime rates. Economic growth remains sluggish despite neoliberal reforms and efforts to attract foreign investment. Recent initiatives include legalizing Bitcoin and pursuing land redistribution to improve food sovereignty. New activists are working to address these issues and seek social and economic justice.

FRANCISCO MARTINEZ

Coffee is often associated with early mornings, late-night work sessions, and a dizzying array of aromas and flavors that captivate coffee connoisseurs. For Francisco Martinez, coffee is a way of life and a source of pride and perseverance.

Although Francisco is currently the administrator of the Marina Cumbre coffee farm, located in the highest part of Cordillera del Bálsamo, the western coastal mountain belt of El Salvador, his journey started as a maintenance man on a coffee farm. He soon worked his way up to manager, overseeing a 350-acre farm. For more than a decade, he would manage several farms and earn certifications attesting to his expertise and passion for coffee.

So, what makes good coffee? For Francisco, it is in the aroma and the variety. He especially likes Red Bourbon and Pacas. Red Bourbon arrived two hundred years ago from Bourbon Island, now called Réunion, which lies close to Madagascar. The Pacas story begins with the discovery of a natural mutation on the Bourbon variety coffee trees on the Pacas family farm in the Santa Ana region of El Salvador in the early twentieth century. The mutation resulted in shorter and more compact coffee trees with smaller leaves. Despite their smaller size, the Pacas trees produced coffee beans of exceptional quality and flavor.

Harvesting the fruits of coffee plants is a delicate and precise practice that requires skill and attention to detail. Only the finest coffee cherries—the bean is a seed inside the red fruit, known as a cherry—are selected and processed. The careful handling of the fruits from the tree to the mill is essential to preserve the unique flavors. Among El Salvador's most celebrated varieties is the award-winning Pacamara, a cross between the Salvadoran Pacas and the Brazilian Maragogipe, developed by the Salvadoran Institute for Coffee Research.

There are different versions of this plant-based drink all over Central and South America. In El Salvador, morro seeds, which come from a tree native to southern Mexico and Central America, are an integral base ingredient. The dried seeds, which are toasted and ground, add a licorice-like flavor to the drink and are believed to carry health benefits that can ease respiratory problems.

HORCHATA DE MORRO

Chilled Rice Drink

**MAKES 4 CUPS BASE,
ENOUGH FOR 8 SERVINGS**

½ cup (4 ounces) dried morro seeds

1 cup long-grain white rice

¾ cup (4 ounces) sesame seeds

6 tablespoons (2 ounces) cocoa nibs

6 tablespoons (2 ounces) skinned natural peanuts

½ cup (2 ounces) pepitas (pumpkin seeds)

2 cinnamon sticks, broken in small pieces

1 tablespoon coriander seeds

½ teaspoon freshly grated nutmeg

4 cups water or nut milk of choice

Superfine sugar for sweetening

Pure vanilla extract for flavoring

Ice cubes

In a large, heavy skillet (preferably cast iron), toast the morro seeds over low heat, stirring occasionally, until they begin to puff, 3 to 4 minutes. Pour into a small bowl and let cool.

Return the skillet to low heat, add the rice, and toast, stirring constantly, until the rice begins to turn golden, 4 to 5 minutes. Add the sesame seeds, cocoa nibs, peanuts, pepitas, cinnamon, and coriander and continue to toast, stirring, until the rice is golden and everything is toasted and fragrant, about 4 minutes more. Pour into a medium bowl and let cool.

In a high-speed blender, combine the toasted morro seeds, toasted rice mixture, and nutmeg, and blend on high until smooth, stopping several times as needed to scrape down the sides of the blender.

Line a fine-mesh sieve with cheesecloth and place over a large bowl. Strain the blended mixture through the sieve, pressing against the solids with the back of a spoon. Gather the corners of the cheesecloth and twist them together to extract every last bit of flavor, then discard the solids. The liquid is your horchata base.

To serve, combine equal parts of the base and water, sweeten to taste with sugar, and add the vanilla to taste. Serve over lots of ice in tall glasses. Leftover base will keep in an airtight container in the refrigerator for up to 1 week.

This refreshing drink can be made with any variety of melon; with a tropical fruit, such as mango or papaya; or with a combination of fruits. Just be sure any fruit you use is ripe and flavorful. This cantaloupe version is particularly bright. Serve it ice cold!

FRESCO DE MELON

Cantaloupe Juice (with or without Rum)

SERVES 4 TO 6

½ cantaloupe, peeled, seeded, and cut into chunks (4 to 5 cups)

4 cups cold water

½ cup superfine sugar

Juice of 2 limes

Ice cubes

1 to 2 ounces dark rum per serving (optional)

In a blender, combine the cantaloupe, water, sugar, and lime juice and blend until smooth. Strain through a fine-mesh sieve into a pitcher. Cover and refrigerate until very cold, 1 to 2 hours.

When ready to serve, fill tall glasses with ice, then add 1 to 2 ounces rum to each glass, if desired. Pour the melon mixture over the ice and serve immediately.

El Salvador boasts one of the highest uses of Worcestershire sauce per capita than any other country in the world, and it makes an appearance here in ceviche, adding a savory note to this otherwise very light everyday first-course tasting dish. Be sure to source the freshest seafood possible.

CEVICHE DE PESCADO Y CAMARÓN

Fish and Shrimp Ceviche

SERVES 4 TO 6

8 ounces medium shrimp, peeled, deveined, and tails removed

8 ounces skinless halibut or red snapper fillet

½ cup freshly squeezed lime juice

Kosher salt

2 plum tomatoes, chopped

½ red onion, finely chopped

2 teaspoons Worcestershire sauce

Hot sauce for seasoning

1 avocado, halved, pitted, peeled, and cut into ½-inch pieces

½ cup coarsely chopped fresh cilantro leaves

Saltine crackers for serving

Cut the shrimp and fish into ½-inch pieces and place in a nonreactive bowl. Pour in the lime juice, season with 1 teaspoon salt, and toss to mix well. Cover and refrigerate for 1 hour, tossing once after 30 minutes. (The fish and shrimp should have "cooked" in the lime juice by this point and turned mostly white.)

Add the tomatoes, onion, and Worcestershire sauce, and season with hot sauce and more salt to taste. Toss well and refrigerate until well chilled and the flavors are blended, 30 minutes to 1 hour.

Just before serving, add the avocado and cilantro and stir and toss gently to mix. Serve at once, with saltines on the side.

This Salvadoran version of an empanada has achiote in the dough, giving it a lively orange color. These turnovers can be filled with meat or chicken or cheese, but this potato version is both very popular and very easy to do.

PASTELITOS DE PAPA

Potato Turnovers

MAKES 12 PASTELITOS

DOUGH

2 cups instant masa harina (such as Maseca brand)

2 teaspoons achiote powder

1 teaspoon chicken bouillon powder

1 teaspoon kosher salt

2 tablespoons melted and cooled lard or vegetable oil

1½ cups water

FILLING

2 large russet potatoes (about 1¼ pounds total)

3 tablespoons vegetable oil

½ green bell pepper, finely chopped

1 small carrot, peeled and finely chopped

1 small yellow onion, finely chopped

2 teaspoons chicken bouillon powder

Kosher salt

½ cup water

Vegetable oil for frying

To make the dough: In a large bowl, combine the masa harina, achiote powder, bouillon powder, and salt and stir and toss with a fork to mix well. Drizzle in the lard and stir and toss to incorporate evenly with the dry ingredients. Drizzle in the water and mix and toss with your hands until the mixture comes together in a smooth, stiff dough that sticks together and is pliable. (If the dough is too crumbly, add a tablespoon or two more water and mix again.) Cover the bowl with plastic wrap and let rest while you make the filling.

To make the filling: In a medium saucepan, combine the potatoes with water to cover and bring to a simmer over medium heat. Simmer until tender all the way through when pierced with a knife, 20 to 30 minutes. Drain the potatoes, let cool, peel, and chop finely.

In a large skillet, heat the oil over medium heat. When the oil is hot, add the bell pepper, carrot, and onion and cook, stirring occasionally, until wilted, 5 to 6 minutes. Season with the bouillon powder and 1 teaspoon salt, add the water, and stir well. Bring to a simmer and cook until the water has almost completely evaporated and the vegetables are tender, 4 to 5 minutes more. Add the potatoes and cook and stir until the mixture comes together, 1 to 2 minutes. Taste and season with salt if needed. Remove from the heat and let cool.

CONTINUED

PASTELITOS DE PAPA

CONTINUED

Divide the dough into twelve equal pieces and roll each piece into a ball. (You can oil your hands to make shaping the balls a little easier.) Lay a plastic sheet on a work surface. (A quart-size ziplock bag that has been split open is the perfect size for this step.) Place a ball on half of the plastic sheet, cover it with the other half, and press down gently to flatten the ball into a disk about 4 inches in diameter and ¼ inch thick. Put 2 to 3 tablespoons of the filling in the center of the round, and fold over to make a half-moon. Using your fingers, press firmly along the edges to seal in the filling. Set the pastelito aside on a large plate or sheet pan. Repeat with the remaining dough balls and filling.

To fry the pastelitos, pour oil to a depth of 1 to 2 inches into a large Dutch oven and heat to 350°F. Line a sheet pan with paper towels and set it near the stove.

When the oil is hot, add half of the pastelitos and fry, turning once, until crisp and a deep orange on both sides, about 3 minutes per side. Using tongs or a wire skimmer, transfer to the towel-lined sheet pan to drain. Let the oil return to 350°F, then fry the remaining pastelitos the same way. Serve hot, warm, or at room temperature.

Somewhere between a soup and a stew, this hearty everyday lunch or dinner is the ultimate comfort food, and although it cooks for 2½ hours, it is easy to put together. If you can't find beef shank, bone-in beef short ribs are a good (though probably more expensive) substitute.

SOPA DE RES

Beef Shank Soup

SERVES 6 TO 8

3 pounds beef shank rounds, 1½ inches thick, or bone-in short ribs, 3-inch pieces

2 bay leaves

4 cups low-sodium beef broth

2 small yellow onions, cut into large chunks

2 carrots, peeled and cut into 1-inch pieces

1 pound cassava or 2 medium russet potatoes, peeled and cut into 1-inch chunks

1 large chayote, peeled and cut into 1-inch-thick wedges

½ small green cabbage, cut into 1-inch-thick wedges

Kosher salt and freshly ground black pepper

2 ears corn, husks and silk removed and each ear quartered crosswise

Lime wedges; finely chopped white or red onion; and chopped fresh cilantro for serving

In a large soup pot or Dutch oven, combine the beef, bay leaves, and broth. Then add water to cover the beef by about 3 inches. Bring to a simmer over medium-high heat. Then turn down the heat to low and simmer uncovered, regularly skimming and discarding any scum that forms on the surface, until the meat is tender, about 2 hours.

Add the onions, carrots, cassava, chayote, and cabbage and continue to simmer until the vegetables are almost tender, about 15 minutes. Taste the broth and season with salt and pepper. Add the corn and simmer until everything is very tender and the meat is almost falling from the bone, 15 to 20 minutes more.

Ladle into bowls and serve with lime wedges, onion, and cilantro on the side for diners to add as they like.

Casamiento means "marriage," and this dish is aptly named, as it's a perfect union of rice and beans. It's often found on breakfast tables in El Salvador but can also be a side dish for roast meats at dinner. This is a quick version made with canned beans, but you can cook your beans from scratch (a pressure cooker is great for this and turns out super-creamy beans). At breakfast, serve this dish alongside eggs, fried plantains, and avocado slices.

CASAMIENTO

Rice and Beans

SERVES 4

2 tablespoons vegetable oil

½ yellow onion, chopped

½ green bell pepper, chopped

1 plum tomato, chopped

1 teaspoon kosher salt

One 15½-ounce can small red beans, drained, with liquid reserved

2 cups cooked long-grain white rice

In a large skillet, heat the oil over medium heat. When the oil is hot, add the onion and bell pepper and cook, stirring occasionally, until wilted, 5 to 6 minutes. Add the tomato and cook, stirring occasionally, until it gives up its juice and begins to break down, 2 to 3 minutes. Season with the salt.

Measure the liquid from the can of beans and add water to equal 1 cup. Add the beans and liquid to the skillet and adjust the heat so the mixture is simmering. Cook until slightly reduced and the sauce is creamy, about 5 minutes. Stir in the rice and continue to cook, stirring and folding constantly, until the mixture dries out slightly and the rice absorbs the cooking juices and turns dark reddish brown, about 5 minutes more. Serve hot.

Pupusas are more than just a food in El Salvador; they are a cultural symbol. They are commonly enjoyed in homes, from street vendors, and in pupuserías (specialty pupusa restaurants) and are often made and shared during family celebrations. The filling can be just beans, beans and cheese, or meat. The cheese is usually quesillo, a semisoft unaged cheese similar to low-moisture mozzarella or Monterey Jack or Mexican queso Oaxaca, any of which can be substituted if you cannot find quesillo. Curtido, a simple cabbage slaw, is the traditional accompaniment.

PUPUSAS CON CURTIDO

Filled Masa Flatbreads with Cabbage Slaw

MAKES 8 PUPUSAS; SERVES 4

CURTIDO

¼ head green cabbage, shredded

1 small carrot, peeled and grated

½ small red onion, thinly sliced

1 small jalapeño chile, sliced and seeded, if desired

4 cups boiling water

¼ cup distilled white vinegar

1 teaspoon kosher salt

1 teaspoon dried oregano

DOUGH

2 cups instant masa harina (such as Maseca brand)

1½ teaspoons kosher salt

1½ cups warm water

FILLING

2 tablespoons lard or vegetable oil

½ small yellow onion, finely chopped

2 cups cooked and drained red beans (such as kidney)

1 teaspoon kosher salt

1 cup water

1 cup shredded quesillo cheese

Vegetable oil for your hands and the griddle

To make the curtido: In a large heatproof bowl, combine the cabbage, carrot, red onion, and chile. Pour in the boiling water, cover the bowl with a large plate, and let sit for 15 minutes. Drain well into a colander, then wipe the bowl dry and return the cabbage mixture to it. Add the vinegar, salt, and oregano and stir and toss to mix well. Cover and refrigerate until chilled and the flavors are blended, at least 1 hour or preferably overnight.

To make the dough: In a large bowl, combine the masa harina and salt and stir and toss with a fork to mix well. Drizzle in the water and mix and toss with your hands until the mixture comes together in a stiff dough. Turn the dough out onto a work surface and knead until it is smooth, not sticky, just until it comes together. Wrap the dough in plastic wrap or a kitchen towel and let rest at room temperature while you make the filling. (The dough can also be made in a stand mixer fitted with the paddle attachment.)

To make the filling: In a medium skillet, heat the lard over medium-low heat. Add the onion and cook, stirring occasionally, until very brown, about 10 minutes. Add the beans, salt, and water, bring to a simmer, and cook, stirring occasionally, until the beans are very creamy and start falling apart, about 10 minutes. Using a potato masher, mash the beans until smooth, then continue to cook, stirring, until very thick, 2 to 3 minutes more. Transfer to a bowl and let cool. Stir in the cheese, mixing well.

CONTINUED

PUPUSAS CON CURTIDO

CONTINUED

To assemble, oil your hands and divide the dough into eight equal pieces. Roll each piece into a ball. Put a ball in the cupped palm of your nondominant hand and, using your dominant hand, make a depression in the center so the ball now resembles a candlestick. Fill the depression with about one-eighth of the filling and press the sides of the ball up and around to enclose the filling. Gently pat the dough into a round about ½ inch thick. Repeat with the remaining dough balls and filling. (If the dough cracks or breaks as you are shaping the rounds, just patch it. If a little filling is showing or leaking through, it's not the end of the world.)

Heat a griddle or a large cast-iron skillet over medium heat. When it is hot, brush it with oil. Working in batches to prevent crowding, lay the pupusas on the griddle and cook until golden brown on the underside, about 3 minutes. Flip and cook until the second side is golden brown, about 3 minutes more. Transfer to a platter. Repeat with the remaining pupusas.

Serve the pupusas warm with the curtido in a bowl on the side.

This crunchy salsa accompanies roasted or grilled meats or starchy dishes like pupusas or can be served as a dip for tortilla or plantain chips. You can also chop the pieces a bit larger and serve the mixture as a side salad. Different variations of this salsa exist across El Salvador and Central America. Some include green or red peppers or cucumber or a bit of heat.

CHIMOL

Radish Salsa

SERVES 4 TO 6

4 plum tomatoes, seeded and chopped

1 bunch radishes (4 to 6 radishes), trimmed and chopped

½ small red onion, chopped

1 teaspoon kosher salt

Juice of 2 limes (about ¼ cup)

1 cup loosely packed fresh cilantro leaves, chopped

In a medium bowl, combine the tomatoes, radishes, and red onion. Sprinkle with the salt and toss well. Add the lime juice and cilantro and toss well again. Cover and refrigerate for at least 1 hour to allow the flavors to blend before serving. The salsa will keep for 2 to 3 days.

This rich, sweet version of rice pudding is easy to make ahead and can be served hot or cold. Some cooks add raisins. If you'd like to do the same, add ½ cup or so for the last few minutes of cooking.

ARROZ CON LECHE

Rice Pudding

SERVES 4 TO 6

3 cups water

1 cinnamon stick

2 strips lemon peel, removed with a vegetable peeler

½ teaspoon kosher salt

1 cup long-grain white rice, rinsed

2 cups whole milk

1 cup sweetened condensed milk

¼ cup sugar, plus more if needed

1 teaspoon pure vanilla extract

2 tablespoons unsalted butter, cut into pieces

Ground cinnamon for serving

In a large saucepan, combine the water, cinnamon stick, lemon peel, and salt, then stir in the rice. Bring to a simmer over medium-low heat and cook, stirring often, until the rice has absorbed the water, about 15 minutes.

Pour in 1 cup of the whole milk and continue to cook, stirring often, until the milk is absorbed, 3 to 5 minutes. Add the remaining 1 cup whole milk and again cook, stirring often, until absorbed, 3 to 5 minutes. Add the condensed milk and sugar and cook, stirring until the sugar has dissolved and the mixture is thick and soupy, 2 to 3 minutes more. (It will thicken more off the heat.) Stir in the vanilla, then taste and add a little more sugar, if desired. Add the butter and stir rapidly to melt and mix well.

Remove from the heat and remove and discard the cinnamon stick and lemon peel. Serve warm in individual bowls, topping each serving with a sprinkle of ground cinnamon. Or let cool to room temperature, then transfer to a covered container and chill.

This unique Salvadoran cake-bread hybrid is both sweet and savory and is eaten at breakfast, as a snack, or as a light dessert. It's traditionally made with queso duro blando, a crumbly, semihard cow's milk cheese, which can be found in the States only in neighborhoods with large Salvadoran communities. Queso Cotija or Parmesan makes a worthy substitute.

QUESADILLA

Sweet Cheese Bread

SERVES 8

1 cup unsalted butter, plus melted butter for the baking dish

1½ cups rice flour

1½ teaspoons baking powder

4 large eggs, separated

1 cup sugar, plus more for sprinkling

¾ cup crema or sour cream

¼ cup whole milk

4 ounces queso duro blando, queso Cotija, or Parmesan cheese, grated on the fine holes of a box grater

2 tablespoons sesame seeds

Preheat the oven to 350°F. Brush the bottom and sides of a 9 by 13-inch baking dish with butter.

In a small bowl, stir together the rice flour and baking powder. In a medium bowl, using an electric mixer, beat the egg whites on medium speed until foamy. With the mixer running, add ½ cup of the sugar in a slow, steady stream and beat until incorporated. Increase the speed to high and beat until the egg whites form soft peaks, 1 to 2 minutes. Set aside.

In a large bowl, using the electric mixer, beat together the remaining ½ cup sugar and the butter on medium speed until creamy. Add the egg yolks, crema, and milk, and beat just until blended. Then add the rice flour mixture and the cheese, and again beat just until fully incorporated. Using a rubber spatula, gently fold in the egg whites in two additions, mixing just until no white streaks remain and being careful to keep the batter light.

Pour the batter into the prepared baking dish. Sprinkle the top evenly with the sesame seeds and a little more sugar. Bake until a toothpick inserted into the center comes out clean, 35 to 40 minutes. Let cool completely on a wire rack. Cut into squares to serve.

IRAQ

LEARN HOW TO PRONOUNCE THE RECIPE NAME

IRAQ

Iraq has always been a point of interest for me. When I was in high school, I boycotted the Iraq War by refusing to get my US citizenship. I've often thought about the complexities of Iraq and how it relates to my beloved Somalia. Again, I think of who gets to tell the story because of time constraints and concerns over safety.

Aline Deschamps, my photographer for Iraq, splits her time between Paris and Beirut. She has ties in Baghdad, which allowed her to move freely to capture the essence of the people of Iraq in a way that added great value to this book.

BACKGROUND

Iraq, officially known as the Republic of Iraq, is bordered by Kuwait, Saudi Arabia, Jordan, Syria, Turkey, and Iran and has a rich history dating back to ancient Mesopotamia, one of the cradles of civilization. The country covers an area of approximately 435,000 square kilometers (167,954 square miles) and has a population of around 46 million people in 2024. Arabic and Kurdish are the official languages, and Baghdad is the capital and largest city.

Iraq is home to diverse ethnic and religious groups. The majority of the population is Arab, while Kurds form a significant minority, particularly in the northern regions. Islam is the dominant religion, with a slight majority of Shia Muslims over Sunni. Iraq can trace its cultural origins back to such ancient civilizations as the Sumerians, Babylonians, and Assyrians, whose contributions to art, science, and literature are widely recognized.

Throughout history, Iraq has witnessed the rise and fall of empires and faced periods of foreign rule. The region was overtaken by various powers, including the Assyrians, Persians, Greeks, Romans, Parthians, Arabs, Mongols,

Following the Gulf War, Iraq faced economic sanctions and continued political challenges. In 2003, a coalition led by the United States invaded Iraq and overthrew the government of Saddam Hussein, citing the alleged presence of weapons of mass destruction. The aftermath of the invasion resulted in a protracted insurgency, sectarian violence, and the rise of extremist groups, including the Islamic State (IS).

Since then, Iraq has been working toward rebuilding its political institutions, security forces, and infrastructure. The country has held multiple elections and established a new constitution but continues to struggle with achieving stability and national reconciliation because of security threats, political divisions, and lagging social and economic development.

2024

Iraq continues to face significant challenges in terms of security, political stability, and economic development. Efforts to rebuild infrastructure, provide essential services, and promote national reconciliation are ongoing. The country's diverse population and regional tensions contribute to complex dynamics and ongoing political divisions. International support and collaboration are crucial for Iraq's path to stability, reconstruction, and sustainable development.

and Ottomans. Following World War I, it came under British control through a League of Nations mandate.

In 1932, Iraq gained independence from Britain and established a constitutional monarchy. However, political instability and military coups marked the country's early years of independence. In 1958, a revolution led to the overthrow of the monarchy, establishing a republican government.

Territorial disputes with neighboring Iran led to the devastating Iran-Iraq War, which began in 1980 and lasted for eight years. Both sides suffered significant casualties and economic damage, and the war ended in a stalemate. In 1990, Iraq invaded Kuwait, leading to the Gulf War, in which an international coalition intervened and forced Iraq to withdraw from Kuwait.

AYAD ASHA

Originally from Baghdad, Ayad Asha has been living in the United States for over a decade, working as a brewer. Home, he explains, is a complex concept due to escaping danger twice; twice, he has had to physically leave his home out of fear for his safety.

Despite this, he finds a sense of home in the company of friends and family rather than in a physical place.

When I ask about Iraqi cuisine, Ayad highlights Masgouf (page 159), a grilled fish dish, as a significant representation of his country's rich culinary heritage. He also mentions such traditional dishes as kubba and dolma, which originated in ancient Mesopotamia (a historical region of West Asia).

Ayad enjoys cooking regularly, finding it to be a fulfilling hobby alongside his passion for soccer and socializing. When I asked Ayad about what's most misunderstood about his beloved country, he expressed frustration with the US media's portrayal of Iraq, which fails to emphasize the welcoming nature of its people, who come from diverse religious and cultural backgrounds.

Ayad tells me passing on food traditions is crucial to him, as it allows him to share his culture and story with others. He describes Iraqi hospitality as generous and inclusive, where offering food and warmth is a common practice.

In terms of community, Ayad values the friendships he has formed in New York, a place in which people from different backgrounds often come together over shared interests like beer, soccer, and music.

Reflecting on his life, Ayad expresses pride in everything he has accomplished. He fondly remembers "home" but is proud of the community and life he has created for himself here in the States.

This hearty dish is a favorite breakfast in Iraq that will keep you happy and full long into the afternoon. Make sure you soak your beans overnight so you're ready to cook first thing in the morning! I'm making fried eggs here, but you can cook scrambled eggs instead. Either way, make sure you have a nice film of olive oil in the bottom of your skillet for both the eggs and the onion, as the name of the dish translates literally as "beans in fat."

BAGILA BIL DIHIN

Fava Beans with Khubz and Fried Eggs

SERVES 4

1 pound dried split fava beans (about 3 cups)

2 garlic cloves, crushed and peeled

Kosher salt and freshly ground black pepper

½ cup extra-virgin olive oil

1 large yellow onion, chopped

4 Khubz | Flatbread (page 165) or pita breads

4 large eggs

Dried mint and chopped tomato for garnish

Lemon wedges for serving

Pick over the favas, discarding any grit or misshapen beans. In a large bowl, combine the favas with water to cover by several inches and soak overnight in the refrigerator. (Unlike dried whole favas, there is no need to peel split favas, as they are sold already peeled.)

The next day, drain the favas and rinse well. In a large saucepan, combine the favas and garlic with water to cover by about 2 inches and bring to a simmer over medium heat. Cook, stirring occasionally, until the favas are creamy and tender, 30 to 45 minutes, depending on the size of the beans. Drain the beans, reserving the cooking liquid. Transfer the beans to a medium bowl and return the cooking liquid to the pan to reheat. Season the beans with salt and pepper.

Heat a large skillet over medium heat and add ¼ cup of the oil. When the oil is hot, add the onion, season with salt and pepper, and cook, stirring often, until the onion is soft and caramelized, 15 to 20 minutes. Transfer the onion and oil to a small bowl and set aside. Wipe out the skillet and reserve.

Meanwhile, using tongs, warm the khubz, one at a time, over the flame of a gas burner, turning as needed, until softened and lightly charred. (Alternatively, you could char the khubz under your electric stove's broiler.) Tear the breads into 1- to 2-inch pieces and divide evenly among four shallow serving bowls.

Ladle about 4 cups favas and liquid over the khubz and then ladle on some of the cooking liquid to moisten. (You'll have leftover cooked favas and liquid. Store them in an airtight container in the refrigerator for up to 4 days. You can dress the beans and liquid with olive oil and herbs for an easy side dish or use them as a base for soup.)

Return the reserved skillet to medium heat and add the remaining ¼ cup oil. When the oil is hot, crack the eggs into the pan and season with salt and pepper. Cook the eggs, basting with the oil, until the whites are set and the yolks are done to your liking.

Transfer a fried egg to each bowl, placing it over favas. Top each serving with one-fourth of the fried onion along with its oil. Garnish with mint and tomato and serve with lemon wedges on the side.

Sumac is the key ingredient in this Iraqi version of a raw vegetable salad that is served as a side for a light lunch. Sumac berries are dried and ground and have a tart, lemony taste that will make your mouth water. They are also prized for their health benefits, which include antioxidant and anti-inflammatory properties.

SALATET SUMMAQ

Sumac Salad

SERVES 4

2 beefsteak tomatoes, chopped, with juices reserved

3 Persian cucumbers, chopped

½ small red onion, thinly sliced

1 cup loosely packed fresh flat-leaf parsley leaves, very roughly chopped

½ cup loosely packed fresh mint leaves, very roughly chopped

2 teaspoons ground sumac, plus more for garnish

2 tablespoons freshly squeezed lemon juice

¼ cup extra-virgin olive oil

Kosher salt and freshly ground black pepper

In a large serving bowl, combine the tomatoes and their juices, cucumbers, onion, parsley, and mint. Sprinkle on the sumac and then toss to mix well. Drizzle with the lemon juice and oil, season with salt and pepper, and toss to coat evenly.

Let the salad sit for 5 to 10 minutes to allow the flavors to mingle before serving. Cover and store any leftover salad in the refrigerator for up to 2 days.

This soup is light yet hearty, and because of that, it's often used to break the fast at Ramadan. Red lentils are split, similar to green split peas, so they cook down and form a creamy consistency on their own—no blender needed.

SHORBAT ADAS

Lentil Soup

SERVES 8

¼ cup extra-virgin olive oil

1 yellow onion, finely chopped

2 cups red lentils, rinsed

2 garlic cloves, finely chopped

2 teaspoons ground cumin

1 teaspoon mild curry powder

½ teaspoon ground turmeric

Kosher salt and freshly ground black pepper

8 cups water

1½ cups dried vermicelli noodles, broken up into short pieces

Fresh flat-leaf parsley leaves for garnish

Lemon wedges for serving

In a large Dutch oven, heat the oil over medium heat. When the oil is hot, add the onion and cook, stirring occasionally, until tender, 7 to 8 minutes. Add the lentils and toss to coat in the oil. Add the garlic, cumin, curry powder, and turmeric and stir to coat the lentils in the spices. Season with 2 teaspoons salt and several grinds of pepper. Pour in the water and bring the mixture to a simmer. Cover with the lid ajar and cook until the lentils are tender and falling apart, about 20 minutes.

Stir in the noodles and simmer just until tender, about 2 minutes. Taste and adjust the seasoning with salt and pepper if needed.

Ladle into individual bowls and top each serving with a sprinkle of parsley. Serve immediately with lemon wedges on the side for squeezing over the top.

In Iraq, this dish is usually made with carp, a hardy and abundant freshwater fish. You can also make it with another freshwater fish, such as tilapia, catfish, or even walleye. It's traditionally cooked over an open fire, but a grill basket and a charcoal grill make this easy to duplicate at home. Have your fishmonger butterfly the fish for you, leaving the head on. Tamarind paste can be found at Asian, Indian, and Latin markets. Once the jar is opened, reseal and keep in the refrigerator.

MASGOUF

Grilled Fish in Tamarind Marinade

SERVES 4

One 2½- to 3-pound whole freshwater fish (see headnote), cleaned and butterflied, with head intact

⅓ cup tamarind paste (see headnote)

2 teaspoons hot curry powder

1½ teaspoons kosher salt

½ teaspoon ground turmeric

¼ cup extra-virgin olive oil, plus more for brushing

1 lemon, halved, plus lemon wedges for serving

Diced tomato, diced red onion, and chopped fresh flat-leaf parsley leaves for finishing

Open the fish, flesh side down, on your work surface, and press gently to flatten. Cut several shallow slits in the skin on both sides to help the marinade penetrate, then flip the fish over. In a medium bowl, stir together the tamarind paste, curry powder, salt, and turmeric until well blended and smooth. Stir in the oil. Transfer the fish to a shallow dish, then pour the marinade over the fish and rub it into both the skin side and the flesh side. Cover the dish and refrigerate for 1 to 2 hours.

Prepare a fire in an outdoor grill (preferably charcoal) for direct cooking over medium heat. Brush the inside of a grill basket large enough to fit the fish with oil. Remove the fish from the refrigerator, squeeze the lemon halves over both sides of the fish, and then put the fish into the basket and secure closed.

Grill the fish skin side down over direct heat until the skin looks charred, about 10 minutes. Flip the basket over and cook flesh side down until the fish flakes when tested with a fork, 6 to 10 minutes more.

Transfer the fish to a platter, top with the tomato, onion, and parsley, and serve immediately, with lemon wedges on the side.

The succulent lamb, slowly cooked to perfection, lends its savory depth to the dish, while the okra adds a delightful textural contrast and a hint of earthy sweetness. Together, they create a harmonious marriage of flavors that is particularly satisfying. This stew is often made with lamb but can also be made with just the okra, a popular vegetable in Iraq, for a vegetarian option. You'll want to make and simmer the sauce first, until it is cooked down and flavored to your liking. If needed, you can add a bit more olive oil to compensate for the lack of animal fat. Add the okra as directed in the recipe. To prepare the okra for stewing, just trim off the tough tops of the stems.

BAMIA

Lamb and Okra Stew

SERVES 4 TO 6

1 pound boneless lamb shoulder, cut into 1-inch chunks

Kosher salt

2 tablespoons extra-virgin olive oil

5 garlic cloves, sliced

⅓ cup tomato paste

2 tablespoons pomegranate molasses

4 plum tomatoes, chopped

3 cups low-sodium chicken or beef broth

1 teaspoon ground coriander

½ teaspoon cayenne pepper

1 pound okra, stem tops trimmed

Cooked long-grain white rice for serving

Season the lamb all over with salt. In a large Dutch oven, heat the oil over medium heat. When the oil is hot, working in batches if needed to avoid crowding, add the lamb chunks and brown on all sides, about 4 minutes per batch. As the lamb is ready, using tongs or a slotted utensil, transfer it to a plate.

Once all of the lamb is browned, add the garlic to the fat remaining in the pot and cook over medium heat, undisturbed until sizzling, about 1 minute. Add the tomato paste and pomegranate molasses and stir. Return the lamb to the pot and add the chopped tomatoes, broth, coriander, cayenne, and 1 teaspoon salt, mixing well. Lower the heat to a simmer, cover with the lid ajar, and cook until the lamb is tender, about 1 hour.

Uncover the pot and add the okra. Increase the heat to medium-high, bring to a rapid simmer, and cook until the okra is tender and the stew has thickened, about 20 minutes. Taste and adjust the seasoning with salt.

Spoon rice onto individual serving plates and top with the stew. Serve immediately.

Iraqi Jews prepare this dish the night before Shabbat. It cooks all night in the oven at a very low temperature (below 250°F) and is served for Shabbat lunch. It is delicious served hot or at room temperature.

TBIT

Slow-Cooked Chicken with Rice

SERVES 4 TO 6

2 cups basmati rice

One 15-ounce can diced tomatoes, with juices

2 tablespoons tomato paste

2 tablespoons Baharat | Spice Blend (page 166)

4 tablespoons extra-virgin olive oil

1 small yellow onion, finely chopped

4 garlic cloves, finely chopped

Kosher salt

1 whole chicken, about 3 pounds

2 cups low-sodium chicken broth

In a medium bowl, combine the rice with water to cover and let soak for 30 minutes.

Preheat the oven to 250°F.

Drain the rice into a fine-mesh sieve and rinse well under cold running water. Transfer the rice to a large bowl, add the canned tomatoes and their juices, tomato paste, baharat, 2 tablespoons of the oil, the onion, garlic, and 1 teaspoon salt, and stir to mix well.

Loosely stuff the cavity of the chicken with about half of the rice mixture and tie the legs together with kitchen twine. Season the outside of the chicken all over with salt.

In a large Dutch oven, heat the remaining 2 tablespoons oil over medium heat. When the oil is hot, carefully add the chicken, breast side down, and brown until the breast is golden, 2 to 3 minutes. Turn the bird breast side up and brown the underside, 2 to 3 minutes more. Spoon the remaining rice mixture around the chicken and spread it evenly. Pour in the broth and bring to a simmer.

Cover the pot, transfer it to the oven, and cook until the chicken and the rice are very tender, 5 to 6 hours.

To serve, carefully transfer the chicken to a platter and snip the twine on the legs. Spoon the rice from the pot around the chicken. Serve hot, warm, or at room temperature.

This simple flatbread is a key component of most Iraqi meals. In Iraq, the breads are often baked in the local equivalent of an Indian tandoor, but you can replicate a similar baking environment at home with a sturdy sheet pan and a very hot conventional oven.

KHUBZ

Flatbread

MAKES 8 FLATBREADS

3½ to 3¾ cups bread flour, plus more for dusting

1 packet (2¼ teaspoons) instant dry yeast

1½ teaspoons kosher salt

1½ cups lukewarm (90° to 100°F) water, plus more if needed

2 tablespoons extra-virgin olive oil, plus more for the bowl and for brushing

Sesame seeds or za'atar for sprinkling

In the bowl of a stand mixer, whisk together 3½ cups of the flour, the yeast, and salt. Add the water and oil, fit the mixer with the paddle attachment, and beat on low speed just until blended. Switch to the dough hook and knead on medium speed until the dough forms a loose ball on the hook and is smooth and springy, 5 to 7 minutes. If the dough seems too dry and crumbly, add more water, about 1 tablespoon at a time. If it seems too wet and sticky, adjust with more flour, about 1 tablespoon at a time.

Oil a large bowl. Gather the dough into a ball, place it in the oiled bowl, and turn the dough to coat on all sides with the oil. Cover the bowl with a kitchen towel and let the dough rise in a warm spot until doubled in size, about 1½ hours.

Line a sheet pan with parchment paper and dust the parchment with flour. Punch the dough down and divide into eight equal pieces. Roll each piece into a ball by stretching the top and tucking the edges under. As the balls are shaped, place them on the prepared sheet pan, spacing them well apart. Lightly cover the sheet pan with plastic wrap and let the balls rise for 20 minutes, until slightly puffy. Meanwhile, position two racks in the center of the oven and preheat the oven to 500°F. Line two sheet pans with parchment paper.

On a clean work surface, using a rolling pin, roll each dough ball into a 6- to 7-inch round about ¼ inch thick and transfer to the prepared sheet pans, spacing the rounds about 1 inch apart. Lightly brush each round with oil and sprinkle with sesame seeds.

Bake the breads, switching the pans between the racks and rotating them back to front at the halfway point, until they puff and are golden brown around the edges, 5 to 7 minutes. Serve hot.

Versions of this warm spice mix exist all over the Middle East. This one is made with pre-ground spices (make sure your spices are very fresh!) and comes together in minutes. If you'd like to use whole spices, just double the amount in the same proportions and toast as directed. Use this earthy, warm spice mixture in Bamia | Lamb and Okra Stew (page 160) or as a rub for roasted meats, fish, or vegetables.

BAHARAT

Spice Blend

MAKES SCANT ½ CUP

2 tablespoons ground cumin

2 tablespoons sweet paprika

1 tablespoon ground coriander

2 teaspoons ground black pepper

1 teaspoon ground cinnamon

1 teaspoon ground cardamom

¼ teaspoon ground nutmeg

¼ teaspoon ground cloves

In a small skillet, combine all the ingredients over low heat and toast, stirring constantly, until the spices are fragrant, 1 to 2 minutes. Pour into a small bowl and let cool before using. Store in a tightly capped glass jar in the pantry for up to 2 months.

This addictive mango condiment is different from the more commonly encountered South Asian sweet mango chutney. It's salty, acidic, funky, and a little sweet. Look for mostly green, firm mangoes to make this recipe. Enjoy it with kebabs, sandwiches, or roasted meat or poultry. You will need to plan ahead when making this condiment, as the salted mangoes must sit for 24 hours before cooking.

AMBA

Pickled Mango Condiment

MAKES ABOUT 2 HEAPING CUPS

2 firm, underripe large mangoes, halved, pitted, peeled, and diced (about 4 cups)

Kosher salt

1 tablespoon extra-virgin olive oil

1 jalapeño chile, seeded, if desired, and finely chopped

3 garlic cloves, finely chopped

1 teaspoon yellow mustard seeds

½ teaspoon ground coriander

½ teaspoon ground cumin

½ teaspoon ground fenugreek

½ teaspoon ground turmeric

½ cup water

¼ cup cider vinegar

2 tablespoons light brown sugar

In a medium nonreactive container, combine the mangoes and 1 tablespoon salt and toss well. Cover and refrigerate for 24 hours.

After 24 hours, in a medium saucepan, heat the oil over medium-low heat. When the oil is hot, add the chile, garlic, and mustard seeds and stir until the mustard seeds begin to pop, 30 seconds to 1 minute. Add the coriander, cumin, fenugreek, and turmeric and stir until fragrant, about 1 minute. Add the mangoes and toss to coat evenly with the spices.

Add the water, vinegar, and brown sugar, stir well, and bring to a simmer, stirring to dissolve the sugar. Cook, stirring occasionally, until the mangoes have softened and are beginning to break down, 5 to 7 minutes. Remove from the heat.

Using an immersion blender, blend the mango mixture to a thick, slightly chunky sauce consistency. Taste and adjust the seasoning with salt if needed. Let cool completely before serving. Store leftovers in a nonreactive airtight container in the fridge for up to several weeks.

Kleicha tamar is the national cookie of Iraq, and for good reason. Home cooks make these yeasted pinwheel cookies for celebratory feasts and holidays, and every family has its own, slightly different recipe. The cookies can also be filled with a pistachio or walnut paste, but the sweet date filling speaks to me the most. The topping of tiny black nigella seeds is more for appearance and can be omitted. If you're working in a very hot kitchen, refrigerate the logs for about 30 minutes before cutting so the filling doesn't ooze out.

KLEICHA TAMAR

Date Cookies

MAKES ABOUT 24 COOKIES

DOUGH

2½ cups all-purpose flour, plus more for rolling

1 tablespoon sugar

¾ teaspoon instant dry yeast

½ teaspoon kosher salt

½ cup unsalted butter, melted and cooled

⅓ cup whole milk

4 tablespoons water, plus more as needed

Extra-virgin olive oil for the bowl

To make the dough: In a stand mixer fitted with the paddle attachment, mix together the flour, sugar, yeast, and salt on low speed just until blended. Drizzle in the butter and milk, then continue to beat on low speed until fully incorporated. Add 3 tablespoons of the water and beat until the mixture comes together in a soft, slightly wet dough. If the dough is still crumbly, add the remaining 1 tablespoon water and beat until blended.

Oil a large bowl. Gather the dough into a ball, place it in the oiled bowl, and turn the dough to coat on all sides with the oil. Cover the bowl with a kitchen towel and let the dough rise in a warm spot until it feels light to the touch, about 45 minutes. The dough won't rise until doubled in size or even rise considerably, but it will feel light and springy when poked.

FILLING

1½ cups pitted dates

1 tablespoon unsalted butter

½ teaspoon ground cardamom

½ cup water

1 large egg yolk beaten with 1 tablespoon whole milk, for egg wash

Nigella seeds for sprinkling (optional)

Meanwhile, make the filling: In a small saucepan, combine the dates, butter, cardamom, and water over low heat and bring to a gentle simmer. Cook until the dates are very soft, 5 to 10 minutes. The timing will depend on how soft the dried dates were. Remove from the heat and let cool, then transfer to a food processor and puree until smooth and spreadable.

Position two racks in the center of the oven and preheat the oven to 350°F. Line two sheet pans with parchment paper.

Divide the dough in half. On a lightly floured work surface, using a rolling pin, roll out half of the dough into an 8 by 12-inch rectangle. Using an offset spatula or the back of a spoon, spread half of the date paste on top, leaving about ½ inch uncovered on all sides. Starting from a long side, roll up the dough into a log. Repeat with the remaining dough and date paste to make a second log.

Brush the top and sides of each log with the egg wash and sprinkle lightly with nigella seeds, if desired. Trim off about ½ inch from the end of each log to expose the pinwheel filling. Cut each log crosswise into twelve equal rounds and place them, spiral side up, on the prepared sheet pans, spacing them about 2 inches apart.

Bake the cookies, switching the pans between the racks and rotating them back to front at the halfway point, until puffed and set to the touch, about 18 minutes. Let cool completely on the pans on wire racks before serving. The cookies will keep in an airtight container at room temperature for up to 3 days.

LEBANO

LEARN HOW TO PRONOUNCE

THE RECIPE NAME

N

LEBANON

Long before I arrive in Lebanon, I see a friend on Instagram enjoying its streets, mountains, and beaches. Quickly, I reach out to him, looking for fixers, community members, and Lebanese citizens living outside the country. He introduces me to a man named Omar Abboud, who is a Lebanese Canadian data scientist and pianist surprisingly based in Brooklyn. We meet for lunch and immediately start to flesh out the details of the trip. Lebanon is much smaller than I anticipated, and Omar is connected in the best way possible. He sends me an email with the subject line "Lebanon List" that includes must-see, must-eat, and must-do things to seek out once I arrive. He also introduces me to Rami Abou-Khalil, an architect who sends me a general guide to all things Lebanon.

Rami's email is vast, and it too includes places to see, foods to eat, and people to talk to. Rami becomes integral to my time on the ground in Lebanon. From his email, it is very clear that he is incredibly proud of his country and is invested in being helpful. Once I'm settled in Beirut, I follow Rami's suggestions closely, helped on my travels by a driver that Omar has suggested.

My trip to Lebanon is on the heels of Thanksgiving in the United States and is the fourth country that I visit on what feels like a whirlwind tour. While I am initially uncertain about my role in narrating the story of Lebanese cuisine, the instant connection formed upon meeting Omar and Rami, coupled with the haunting call of prayer, begins to resonate within me. At this moment, I sense the intricate tapestry of complexities that defines the essence of Lebanon.

BACKGROUND

Officially known as the Lebanese Republic, Lebanon is bordered by Syria to the north and east and Israel to the south. It has a varied cultural heritage and a diverse population. The country covers an area of approximately 10,500 square kilometers (4,054 square miles) and had a population of around 5.5 million in 2022. Arabic is the official language, and Beirut is the capital as well as the largest city.

Lebanon has a complex ethnic and religious makeup. The population includes various religious communities, such as Muslims (Sunni, Shia, and others), Christians (Maronite, Greek Orthodox, and others), and Druze. This diversity has contributed to Lebanon's unique cultural and political landscape.

Throughout history, Lebanon has experienced numerous periods of foreign rule and conflict. In ancient times, it was controlled by the Phoenicians, conquered by Alexander the Great, and later became a Roman province. Beginning in the Middle Ages, it fell under the control of a long list of powerful occupiers, including the Byzantines, the Arabs, the Crusaders, the Mamluks, and the Ottomans.

With the 1920 partition of the Ottoman Empire following its defeat in World War I, Lebanon was placed under French control. In the years that followed, it saw the rise of nationalistic movements and demands for independence. In 1943, Lebanon achieved autonomy from France and established a political system known as confessionalism. It distributed power among the primary religious communities, with the position of president reserved for a Maronite Christian, the prime minister for a Sunni Muslim, and the speaker of the parliament for a Shia Muslim.

Despite independence, Lebanon has faced ongoing challenges, including political instability, sectarian tensions, and external interventions. The country experienced a crippling civil war from 1975 to 1990, which resulted in significant loss of life, a broken economy, and hundreds of thousands of displaced civilians. The war involved multiple factions, including sectarian militias and foreign powers.

In recent years, Lebanon has grappled with a range of crises, including economic downturns, political gridlock, and social unrest. The country faces high levels of public debt, corruption, and widespread socioeconomic inequalities. In 2020, Lebanon went through a severe economic crisis characterized by a currency devaluation, hyperinflation, and large-scale protests against the government.

2024

Lebanon continues to face significant challenges in terms of political stability, economic recovery, and social cohesion. The country's infrastructure and institutions require rebuilding, and efforts to address corruption and sectarian divisions are ongoing. Lebanon also continues to host an estimated 1.5 million refugees from Syria, further straining its resources and infrastructure. International support and efforts toward political and economic reforms are crucial for Lebanon's path to stability and prosperity.

MIKEY MUHANNA

Beirut resident Mikey Muhanna is the founder of Afikra, an organization dedicated to promoting curiosity and connection in the Arab world. With a mission to encourage individuals to reconsider the histories and cultures of the region, Mikey provides a space for critical thinking and reframing perceptions of the past, present, and future of the Middle East. When I asked Mikey about the concept of community, he said it revolves around a group of individuals invested in one another's past, present, and future. They come together to pursue personal growth while cherishing the present and the past. Mikey believes that communities should support and serve one another, creating an environment where individuals can authentically express themselves and explore their true identities.

He takes immense pride in his relationships with his biological family and his chosen family. He values the iterative love and commitment involved in understanding and supporting others in becoming their best selves. Mikey extends this philosophy to Afikra, aiming to create a supportive network of individuals reimagining their place in the world and working together to shape a better future.

To Mikey, "home" represents a place in which unfiltered community thrives. It is characterized by open doors where individuals can engage with one another without reservation or fear of judgment. The essence of home lies in the warmth and acceptance shared among individuals, enabling them to be fully present in one another's company, he says.

When discussing Beirut, Mikey draws parallels to such other multidimensional cities as New Orleans. He describes Beirut as a place that offers a multitude of experiences, both inspiring and challenging. He says it stimulates the senses with vibrant energy and a visually captivating environment. Mikey acknowledges that Beirut may not appeal to everyone, as it requires a specific type of person who appreciates exploring contradictions and making sense out of seemingly opposing elements. Living in Beirut means being a caretaker of its rich cultural heritage while navigating the complexities of its diverse population.

Mikey concludes our interview by emphasizing the heterogeneity of Lebanon and his preference for focusing on cities rather than states. He believes that cities embody a sense of identity that transcends geopolitical boundaries.

Lebanese cabbage rolls are smaller and thinner than those found in most other countries, so they can be eaten as a first or second course, depending on how many you serve. These rolls can also be prepared without meat. Just add some vegetables (carrots or more onion slices work well) to the mix or ½ cup or so of rinsed brown lentils. Take care not to shape the rolls too tightly or to jam them too close together in the pot because the rice expands quite a bit.

MALFOUF

Cabbage Rolls

MAKES ABOUT 15 ROLLS; SERVES 4 TO 6

Kosher salt

1 large green cabbage

1½ cups short-grain white rice

1 pound ground beef or lamb

¼ cup chopped fresh flat-leaf parsley

3 garlic cloves chopped, plus 4 garlic cloves, sliced

2 teaspoons Baharat | 7 Spice Mix (page 203)

6 tablespoons extra-virgin olive oil, plus more for drizzling

1 small yellow onion, sliced

4 cups low-sodium chicken broth

Juice of 2 lemons

1 teaspoon dried mint

Lemon wedges for serving

Bring a large pot of salted water to boil. Cut the core out of the cabbage and separate the leaves. Select as many large, whole leaves as you can (about fifteen), then shred the remainder of the cabbage. Add the whole leaves to the boiling water and boil just until floppy, about 5 minutes. Drain into a colander, then rinse under cold running water until cool and drain again. Lay the leaves, rib side up, on a cutting board and, using a sharp paring knife, carefully pare down the ribs.

To make the filling: In a large bowl, combine the rice, meat, parsley, chopped garlic, spice mix, and 2 teaspoons salt and mix with your hands until well blended.

Lay the cabbage leaves trimmed-rib side down. Roll about 3 tablespoons of the filling into a sausage shape, set it about 1 inch up from the bottom of a leaf, fold the bottom up over the filling, fold in the sides, and roll up like a little burrito. (Don't roll *too* tightly or they'll bust open as the rice expands.) Repeat with the remaining leaves and filling. (If you have a few extra leaves, shred them. If you have a little extra filling, make a few small meatballs. Add the shredded leaves or meatballs to the pot when you cook the rolls.)

CONTINUED

MALFOUF

CONTINUED

Add 3 tablespoons of the oil to a large Dutch oven, distributing it evenly over the bottom, and then scatter in the sliced garlic, onion, and shredded cabbage. Add the rolls in one or two layers, depending on the size of your pot. Combine the broth and lemon juice in a spouted measuring cup and stir in 1 teaspoon salt. Pour over the rolls. The liquid should almost cover them. If it doesn't, add water as needed. Drizzle with the remaining 3 tablespoons oil and sprinkle with the mint. Place a heatproof plate on top of the rolls to weigh them down and keep them from floating. Bring to a gentle simmer over low or medium-low heat, cover, and cook until the cabbage is very tender—just pierce a leaf with a knife to make sure—1 to 1¼ hours.

Serve warm or at room temperature, with lemon wedges on the side.

Kibbeh is a mixture of ground meat and a grain, usually bulgur. There are endless variations of kibbeh in Lebanon, both raw and cooked, but this one is both simple and stellar because it highlights the quality of the ingredients. It can be made with beef, lamb, or veal (I'm using lamb here). Make sure whichever meat you choose is perfectly fresh and is not ground until you're ready to put the dish together.

KIBBEH NAYEH

Raw Kibbeh

SERVES 4 TO 6

1 pound boneless lamb from leg, cut into small chunks

½ cup fine bulgur

4 ice cubes

½ small white onion, cut into chunks, plus more finely chopped for serving

1 teaspoon Baharat | 7 Spice Mix (page 203)

1½ teaspoons kosher salt

¼ cup loosely packed fresh mint leaves

Extra-virgin olive oil, for drizzling

Pita bread or raw vegetables (such as carrot, celery, cucumber, or bell pepper) for serving

Put the lamb into the freezer for 30 minutes before you begin. Chill a serving platter in the refrigerator.

In a medium bowl, combine the bulgur with water to cover by several inches. Let soak until softened, 15 to 20 minutes. Drain the bulger in a fine-mesh sieve and press against it with the back of a spoon to extract as much water as possible. Set aside.

Scatter the chilled lamb cubes in a food processor and add the ice cubes. Process until the meat is an almost-smooth paste, 2 to 3 minutes. Transfer to a large bowl. Add the onion chunks, spice mix, and salt to the food processor and process until the onion is very finely chopped. Add the onion mixture and the bulgur to the bowl with the lamb. Using wet hands, mix everything together until very well blended, 2 to 3 minutes. Cover and chill the mixture for 15 minutes.

Remove the platter from the refrigerator. Turn the kibbeh out onto the platter and flatten it into a large patty in the center. Use the back of a spoon to press little ridges on top. Tear the mint leaves, dropping them onto the kibbeh. Drizzle with oil and finish with a sprinkle of finely chopped onion. Serve with pita or vegetables (or just forks!).

This crispy fried cauliflower can be an appetizer, a snack, or a sandwich or pita filling, plus it's great hot or at room temperature. While frying is the traditional cooking method, you could also prepare it in a very hot oven or an air fryer.

ARNABEET MEKLEH

Fried Cauliflower with Tahini

SERVES 4

Vegetable oil for frying

½ cup tahini, at room temperature

Juice of 1 lemon

1 garlic clove, very finely chopped

⅓ cup water

½ large head cauliflower, cut into florets

Kosher salt

Lemon wedges for serving

Pour oil to a depth of about 2 inches into a large Dutch oven and heat to 365°F. Line a sheet pan with paper towels and set it near the stove.

While the oil heats, in a small bowl, whisk together the tahini, lemon juice, and garlic. Whisk in the water until the sauce is smooth and creamy. Set aside until serving.

When the oil is ready, add the cauliflower and cook, turning the florets as needed to color evenly and adjusting the heat if necessary to maintain the oil at 365°F, until the cauliflower is tender and deep golden brown, 4 to 5 minutes. Using a wire skimmer, transfer to the towel-lined sheet pan to drain and immediately season with salt.

Serve the warm cauliflower with the tahini sauce for dipping and lemon wedges on the side.

This dish features triple carbs, making it great Lebanese comfort food. It also has double pomegranate—molasses and arils. It is traditionally made with fresh pasta strands, but dried pasta works almost as well and eliminates a step. Additionally, it's a popular Syrian dish, reflecting the shared culinary traditions between Lebanon and Syria that lead to crossover dishes enjoyed by both countries.

HARAK OSBAO

Lentils with Crispy Pita and Pomegranate

SERVES 4 TO 6

1 pita bread with pocket

7 tablespoons extra-virgin olive oil

6 ounces long, flat dried pasta (such as linguine or fettuccine), broken into 2- to 3-inch lengths

2 large yellow onions, sliced

Kosher salt

6 cups water, plus more if needed

2 cups brown lentils, rinsed

3 tablespoons pomegranate molasses, plus more for drizzling

1 cup loosely packed fresh cilantro leaves

2 garlic cloves, crushed and peeled

⅓ cup pomegranate arils (seeds)

Ground sumac for garnish

Lemon wedges for serving

Preheat the oven to 350°F. Split the pita bread into two rounds, then tear the rounds into roughly 1-inch pieces. Pile the pieces on a sheet pan, drizzle with 1 tablespoon of the oil, and toss to coat evenly. Spread the pieces in a single layer on the pan, transfer to the oven, and toast until crisp and golden, 8 to 10 minutes. Set aside.

In a large skillet, heat 1 tablespoon of the oil over medium-low heat. When the oil is hot, scatter the pasta pieces in the pan and cook, stirring constantly, until lightly toasted, 2 to 3 minutes. Transfer to a bowl and set aside.

In the same skillet, heat 3 tablespoons of the oil over medium-low heat. When the oil is hot, add the onions, season with salt, and cook, stirring occasionally, until they are deep golden and soft, 20 to 25 minutes. Set aside until serving.

While the onions are cooking, in a large saucepan or Dutch oven, combine the water, lentils, pomegranate molasses, and 2 teaspoons salt and bring to a simmer over medium-low heat. Simmer, stirring occasionally, until the lentils are just beginning to lose their bite, about 20 minutes. Add the toasted pasta and continue to simmer until most of the water is absorbed and the lentils and pasta are tender, about 10 minutes more. (The mixture should still be slightly soupy at this point. The lentils and pasta will absorb more liquid off the heat.) If the pan begins to dry out before the lentils and pasta

CONTINUED

HARAK OSBAO

CONTINUED

are ready, add another cup or so of water. Stir in the remaining 2 tablespoons oil, then taste and adjust the seasoning with salt if needed.

Pile the cilantro and garlic on a cutting board and chop together very finely. Transfer the lentils and pasta to a shallow serving bowl. Top with the onions, cilantro-garlic mixture, pomegranate arils, and pita crisps. Sprinkle with sumac, drizzle with pomegranate molasses, and serve, with lemon wedges on the side.

Maghmour is not just a dish. It's a representation of cultural identity, regional diversity, and the values of Middle Eastern cuisine. It reflects a deep connection to the land, traditions, and the importance of gathering around a table to share flavorful and satisfying food with loved ones. This traditionally vegan dish can be served hot or at room temperature as either a side or a main. Although not essential, peeling the eggplants in a stripe pattern will help the cubes cook up faster and more tender and will keep them from falling apart in the sauce.

MAGHMOUR

Eggplant and Chickpea Stew

SERVES 4 TO 6

2 medium eggplants (about 2 pounds total)

6 tablespoons extra-virgin olive oil

Kosher salt

1 yellow onion, chopped

3 garlic cloves, chopped

1 teaspoon ground cumin

½ teaspoon ground cinnamon

¼ teaspoon cayenne pepper

One 15-ounce can diced tomatoes, with juices

1½ cups water

Two 15-ounce cans chickpeas, drained and rinsed

Dried mint for finishing

Preheat the oven to 400°F.

Using a vegetable peeler, and working lengthwise, remove the peel from the eggplants in a stripe pattern, then cut the eggplant into about 1½-inch cubes. Pile the cubes on a large sheet pan, drizzle with 3 tablespoons of the oil, sprinkle with 1 teaspoon salt, and toss to coat evenly. Spread the cubes in a single layer.

Roast the eggplant cubes, tossing once halfway through, until golden and just tender, about 20 minutes.

While the eggplant roasts, in a medium Dutch oven, heat the remaining 3 tablespoons oil over medium heat. Add the onion and cook, stirring occasionally, until softened, about 8 minutes. Add the garlic, cumin, cinnamon, and cayenne and let sizzle undisturbed for 1 minute. Add the diced tomatoes and their juices, then add 1 cup of the water to the tomato can, swirl to release any tomato residue, and add to the pot. Bring to a simmer and cook, stirring occasionally, until the sauce begins to thicken, 5 to 7 minutes.

Add the roasted eggplant, chickpeas, and the remaining ½ cup water to the sauce, bring to a simmer, and cook until the mixture is thick and flavorful and the eggplant is quite soft, 10 to 15 minutes more. Sprinkle with mint just before serving from the pot.

This dish is popular in late spring, before the weather gets too hot and the dandelion greens grow too bitter. It can be served as a first course or a side dish.

HINDBEH B'ZEIT

Braised Dandelion Greens with Caramelized Onions

SERVES 4 TO 6

Kosher salt

2 large bunches dandelion greens, tough stems trimmed (about 2 pounds)

4 tablespoons extra-virgin olive oil

2 large yellow onions, sliced

Kosher salt

2 garlic cloves, chopped

½ lemon

Bring a large pot of salted water to boil. Add the greens and cook until just tender, 8 to 10 minutes. Drain into a colander and rinse under cold running water until cool. Let drain, then squeeze out any excess water with your hands. Set aside.

In a large skillet, heat 3 tablespoons of the oil over medium-low heat. Add the onions and toss to coat in the oil. Season with 1 teaspoon salt and cook, stirring often, until deep golden, 15 to 18 minutes. Transfer half of the onions to a small bowl.

Add the remaining 1 tablespoon oil to the skillet and then add the garlic and increase the heat to medium-high. Once the garlic and onions are sizzling, after about 1 minute, add the greens and 1 teaspoon salt and cook, stirring and tossing occasionally, until the greens give up any excess liquid and the liquid evaporates, 3 to 5 minutes.

Remove from the heat, squeeze the lemon half over the greens, and toss to mix. Transfer to a serving dish, top with the reserved onions, and serve.

Sometimes called "purse bread" because it's shaped like a handbag with a short strap, this is quintessential street food to be eaten on the go or at home for breakfast or a snack with a cup of tea. The breads are usually baked in a wood-fired oven, but the addition of a couple of tablespoons of sugar to the dough here helps replicate the crusty exterior of the traditionally crunchy bread rings. Although they are delicious plain, they're also often split and filled with labne and a sprinkle of za'atar.

KAAK

Sesame Bread Rings

SERVES 4

2½ cups all-purpose flour, plus more for the work surface

2 tablespoons sugar

2 teaspoons instant dry yeast

1½ teaspoons kosher salt

¾ cup whole milk, at room temperature

½ cup water, at room temperature, plus more if needed

2 tablespoons extra-virgin olive oil, plus more for the bowl

1 large egg, beaten, for egg wash

2 tablespoons sesame seeds

In the bowl of a stand mixer, whisk together the flour, sugar, yeast, and salt. In a spouted measuring cup, stir together the milk, water, and oil. Fit the mixer with the paddle attachment, add the milk mixture to the flour mixture, and beat on low speed just until blended. Switch to the dough hook and continue to beat on low speed just until the dough comes together in a shaggy ball. It should be loose and somewhat wet; if it's still crumbly, add more water, a tablespoon at a time, and beat on low speed until the dough is no longer too dry. Increase the speed to medium-high and beat until the dough forms a smooth, loose ball on the hook, 5 to 6 minutes.

Transfer the dough to a floured work surface, knead a few times to bring it together, and then gather into a ball. Oil a large bowl, place the dough in the bowl, and turn the dough to coat on all sides with the oil. Cover the bowl with a kitchen towel and let the dough rise in a warm spot until doubled in size, about 1 hour.

CONTINUED

KAAK

CONTINUED

Line two sheet pans with parchment paper. Punch the dough down and divide into four equal pieces. Shape each piece into a ball by stretching the top and tucking the edges under. Place a ball on a clean work surface and use your palms to flatten it into an oval that is slightly larger at the bottom than at the top (about 8 inches long at its longest point) and is a scant ½ inch thick. Use a small round biscuit or cookie cutter (2 inches or so in diameter) or overturned drinking glass to cut a round of dough from the top of each oval. Transfer the oval and the cutout to a prepared sheet pan. Repeat with the remaining dough balls, arranging two ovals and cutouts on each pan. Loosely cover the pans with plastic wrap and let the dough rise until almost doubled in size, 30 to 40 minutes.

About 20 minutes before the dough is ready, position two racks in the center of the oven and preheat the oven to 450°F.

When the breads are ready to bake, brush the tops with the egg wash and sprinkle evenly with the sesame seeds. Bake the breads, switching the pans between the racks and rotating them back to front halfway through, until they are dark golden all over and crisp on the bottom, 8 to 10 minutes. Transfer to wire racks to cool to room temperature before serving. These are best enjoyed the day they are made, or wrap in foil and keep for 1 to 2 days at room temp.

These meat-stuffed pitas, which are typically enjoyed as a quick lunch, a snack, or on-the-go street food, can be filled with beef or lamb. Whatever meat you choose, make sure you use a lean cut so the fat doesn't seep out and make the bread soggy. If you like, you can slice each stuffed pita in half after cooking for a snack- or appetizer-size serving.

ARAYES

Meat-Stuffed Pitas

MAKES 12 STUFFED PITA HALVES

1 small yellow onion, coarsely chopped

4 garlic cloves, crushed and peeled

½ cup loosely packed fresh cilantro leaves

½ cup loosely packed fresh flat-leaf parsley leaves

¼ cup pine nuts, toasted

1½ pounds lean ground beef or lamb

1 tablespoon Baharat | 7 Spice Mix (page 203)

1½ teaspoons kosher salt

6 pita breads with pockets, halved

Extra-virgin olive oil for cooking

Tahini for serving

Lemon wedges for serving

In a mini food processor, combine the onion, garlic, cilantro, parsley, and pine nuts and pulse until a chunky paste forms. Transfer the paste to a large bowl, add the meat, spice mix, and salt, and mix with your hands until well blended.

Place a sheet pan in the oven and preheat the oven to its lowest setting. Divide the meat mixture into twelve equal portions and stuff a portion into each pita half, pressing to flatten slightly.

Preheat a large cast-iron skillet over medium heat and brush liberally with oil. Add as many pita halves as will fit in a single layer without crowding and cook until crisp and golden on the underside, about 4 minutes. Flip and repeat on the second side, 3 to 4 minutes more. Transfer to the sheet pan and keep warm in the oven. Repeat with the remaining pita halves.

Serve hot with tahini for dipping and lemon wedges on the side.

200

Grape Molasses
500 g
72,000 LL

Grape
Syrup
60,000 LL

Grape Syrup
60,000 LL

Grape dressing
120,000 LL

Olivado chili
Spicy Jam
356,000 LL

Olivado
apple chutney
311,000 LL

Olivado
Pumpkin butter
235,000 LL

Nabaty
Tabasco
104,000 LL

Nabaty
Habanero oil
178 LL

Nabaty paste
120,000 LL

Nabaty thai
flakes
104,000 LL

Habanero
flakes
113,000 LL

Chili paste
135,000 LL

Pickle
pickles
134,000 LL

Vine leaves
188,000 LL

pickled wild
thyme
183,000 LL

Bamyeh
in oil
97,000 LL

Zaatar
shanklish
133,000 LL

Spicy
shanklish
250,000 LL

Olives stuffed
with labne
178,000 LL

Kashek w
a Khdar
230,000 LL

BREAD & BUTTER
PICKLES

While all of the spice blends of the Middle East in this book may seem similar, each has its own unique flavor. A healthy dose of allspice takes this blend in a warm, almost-sweet direction.

BAHARAT

7 Spice Mix

MAKES A HEAPING ½ CUP

2 tablespoons ground allspice

2 tablespoons ground coriander

2 tablespoons ground cinnamon

1 tablespoon ground cloves

1 tablespoon ground cumin

1 tablespoon ground nutmeg

1 tablespoon freshly ground black pepper

In a small skillet, combine the allspice, coriander, cinnamon, cloves, cumin, and nutmeg over low heat and toast, stirring constantly, until the spices are fragrant, about 2 minutes. Pour into a small bowl, stir in the pepper, and let cool before using. Store in a tightly capped glass jar in the pantry for up to 2 months.

This bright, slightly sweet dip is a Lebanese classic and is a good partner with other creamy dips, such as labne or hummus, as part of a meze offering. It can be made a few days ahead and refrigerated in an airtight container, then brought to room temperature before serving. Use warm pita bread or crunchy raw vegetables for dipping.

MOUHAMARA

Spicy Walnut and Red Pepper Dip

SERVES 4 TO 6

2 large red bell peppers

1 slice good-quality whole-wheat bread, tough crusts removed

½ cup walnuts, toasted

1 Fresno chile, seeded, if desired, and chopped

2 tablespoons pomegranate molasses, plus more for drizzling

Juice of ½ lemon

1½ teaspoons kosher salt

3 tablespoons extra-virgin olive oil

Using tongs, one at a time, turn the peppers over the flame of a gas burner until the skin blisters and the peppers are evenly charred on all sides. (If you have an electric stove, use the broiler to blister and char the peppers.) Transfer the peppers to a medium bowl, cover with plastic wrap, and steam until cooled, about 15 minutes.

Peel the charred skin from the cooled peppers. Then slit the peppers open, remove and discard the stems and seeds, and cut into coarse chunks.

Tear the bread into rough chunks, drop into a food processor, and pulse to fine crumbs. You should have about ½ cup.

Leave the bread crumbs in the food processor, add the bell pepper chunks, walnuts, chile, pomegranate molasses, lemon juice, and salt, and pulse until a chunky paste forms. With the processor running, slowly drizzle in the oil to create an almost-smooth dip. (If the dip is too thick, thin with a tablespoon or two of water.)

Transfer the dip to a serving bowl, drizzle with pomegranate molasses, and serve.

The combination of turmeric and semolina flour gives this simple cake a beautiful sunny yellow hue and slightly nutty flavor. It is unusual in that it contains no eggs or butter, and if you'd like to make a vegan version, you need only substitute your favorite plant-based milk for the whole milk. Sfouf is often enjoyed as a dessert or snack alongside a cup of tea or coffee, particularly during festive occasions and family gatherings.

SFOUF

Semolina Turmeric Cake

SERVES 6 TO 8

½ cup canola oil, plus more for the baking pan

1 cup fine semolina flour

1 cup all-purpose flour

1½ teaspoons ground turmeric

1½ teaspoons baking powder

¼ teaspoon kosher salt

1 cup sugar

1 cup whole milk

¼ cup pine nuts (optional)

Preheat the oven to 350°F. Brush an 8-inch round baking pan with oil.

In a medium bowl, sift together the semolina and all-purpose flours, turmeric, baking powder, and salt. In a large bowl, whisk together the sugar and oil until smooth. Whisk in the milk until well blended. Add the flour mixture to the milk mixture and whisk just until blended. Transfer the batter to the prepared baking pan. Sprinkle the top with the pine nuts, if using.

Bake the cake until a toothpick inserted into the center comes out with just a few crumbs attached, 30 to 35 minutes. Let cool completely on a wire rack. Cut into squares or diamonds to serve.

LIBERIA

LEARN HOW TO PRONOUNCE THE RECIPE NAME

LIBERIA

After my journey to Congo, I ventured into Liberia, and the two countries couldn't have been more distinct. Traveling between African nations always presents its own set of challenges. The intracontinental journey between Congo and Liberia took an unexpected turn when Riley and I found ourselves stuck in Conakry, Guinea, for a night, causing a delay in our plans. Despite the hurdles and a full day of travel, we finally landed in Monrovia, Liberia.

On arrival, I felt a sense of relief wash over me as we were greeted in the immigration line by a friend of a friend, ready to pick us up. Liberia immediately embraced me with a comforting atmosphere and an unmistakable sense of ease.

BACKGROUND

Liberia, officially known as the Republic of Liberia, is located on the western coast of Africa. It shares a border with Sierra Leone, Guinea-Conakry, and Côte d'Ivoire. The country spans approximately 111,369 square kilometers (around 43,000 square miles). The population numbers approximately 5.6 million, and Liberia is known for its diverse ethnic groups, with the largest being the Kpelle, Bassa, Gio, Mano, and Grebo people. The official language in Liberia is English, which explains why recipe titles are in English. Moreover, Liberian Kreyol, a creole language, is

commonly spoken alongside the country's twenty indigenous languages.

The Liberian economy mainly depends on natural resources like iron ore, rubber, timber, and palm oil, but there are ongoing efforts to diversify into sectors like agriculture and services such as tourism, transportation, and telecommunications. Liberia has a complex history that includes periods of colonization, slavery, and civil conflict. It was founded in the early nineteenth century by

formerly enslaved African Americans and free-born African Americans who returned to Africa under the auspices of the American Colonization Society. The capital city, Monrovia, was named after James Monroe, the fifth president of the United States.

Liberia endured fourteen years of civil war, which ended in 2003. In 2006, Liberia became the first country in Africa to elect a female president, Ellen Johnson Sirleaf, who, along with a group of women, played a crucial role in brokering the peace treaty that ended the conflict. Throughout its history, Liberia has faced challenges related to governance, social inequality, and economic development. The country has a significant wealth gap, with a small elite class holding much of the capital while many citizens live in poverty. Liberia has struggled with political instability, corruption, and the aftermath of civil wars.

2024

Liberia has faced significant stresses throughout its history, including periods of political unrest, civil wars, and economic downturns. The country has made progress in rebuilding and restoring stability, but there is still work to be done in addressing such issues as wealth inequality and corruption. Liberia continues to strive for sustainable development, democratic governance, and the well-being of its people.

TANYA ANSAHTA GARNETT

Tanya Ansahta Garnett is a versatile individual with a diverse array of talents and passions. As a restaurateur, chef, professor, and singer-songwriter, she wears many hats and endeavors to integrate these varied facets of her identity into her work. Born in Boston to Liberian parents, Tanya has navigated between her two cultural backgrounds, finding ways to harmonize them throughout her life.

Upon returning to Liberia a decade ago after living in New Orleans, Tanya found herself drawn to combining her various skills and interests. She often hosts dinners that serve as a platform for her professional network, bringing together individuals from different backgrounds, ranging from university academics and embassy officials to local Liberians. At these gatherings, she not only showcases her culinary expertise but also fosters meaningful connections among people.

Tanya's entrepreneurial spirit is evident in her approach to cooking, where she blends her knowledge of international cuisine with a deep commitment to local produce and sustainable agricultural practices. Through her culinary creations, she seeks to highlight the political and cultural significance of food in Liberia. For instance, her emphasis on using only locally grown rice reflects a broader narrative of self-sufficiency and resistance against imported goods.

Drawing parallels between her experiences living in New Orleans from 2004 to 2012 and Liberia, Tanya reflects on the cultural heritage and linguistic influences shared by the two places. She underscores the historical connections between African and African American communities, highlighting the enduring legacy of migration and cultural exchange across the Atlantic.

In her exploration of Liberian cuisine, Tanya is passionate about reviving traditional cooking techniques and preserving culinary customs. She emphasizes the importance of embracing the roughness and authenticity of Liberian food, which often reflects the resourcefulness and resilience of the country's people. Despite the challenges posed by limited access to certain ingredients, Tanya remains committed to showcasing the richness and diversity of Liberian cuisine.

Through her work as a chef, educator, and cultural ambassador, Tanya endeavors to challenge stereotypes and misconceptions about Liberia. She believes in the power of food to foster understanding and connection across cultures, inviting others to explore the vibrant culinary traditions of her homeland.

This is my simple, homemade version of a delicious and refreshing drink available all over Liberia. Use the freshest ginger you can find to extract the most juice and flavor. You can add cold seltzer in place of the water to make an at-home version of ginger beer.

PINEAPPLE GINGER JUICE

MAKES ABOUT 8 CUPS

12 ounces fresh ginger, peeled and cut into chunks

1 pineapple, peeled, quartered lengthwise, cored, and cut into chunks

Juice of 1 lemon

½ teaspoon ground allspice

¼ teaspoon ground cloves

1 cup sugar, plus more if needed

6 cups water

Ice cubes for serving

Line a large fine-mesh sieve with cheesecloth and set over a large bowl. In a second large bowl, combine the ginger, pineapple, lemon juice, allspice, and cloves. Sprinkle the sugar over everything and toss to mix well.

Depending on the size of your blender, you can blend the ginger-pineapple mixture in two or three batches. Transfer a batch to the blender, add 2 cups of the water if blending one-third and 3 cups of the water if blending half, and blend the mixture until very smooth. Pour into the cheesecloth-lined sieve and press against the solids with the back of a spoon to extract as much liquid as possible. Repeat with the remaining mixture and water in one or two batches, straining each batch as directed. Discard the solids.

Taste the juice. It should have a nice balance of sweet, spicy, and acidic. Add sugar to taste if needed. The juice should have the consistency of orange juice. If it is too thick, add a bit more water. Transfer to a pitcher, cover, and refrigerate until well chilled. Serve over lots of ice.

In Liberia, this main dish soup, eaten at lunch or dinner, is made with just about any protein—beef, chicken, or fish. I'm using poultry here because it cooks relatively quickly and is less costly than beef or fish. You can add more or fewer Scotch bonnets, depending on your tolerance for heat. If you'd like to make this more substantial, you can add some okra or eggplant in the last 20 minutes or so of cooking.

GROUND PEANUT SOUP

SERVES 4

3 tablespoons vegetable oil

2 pounds bone-in, skin-on chicken thighs

Kosher salt and freshly ground black pepper

1 smoked turkey neck

1 medium yellow onion, halved, then half chopped and half cut into chunks

6 cups water

2 plum tomatoes, coarsely chopped

2-inch piece fresh ginger, peeled and coarsely chopped

4 garlic cloves, crushed and peeled

2 tablespoons tomato paste

1 teaspoon sweet paprika

4 cups low-sodium chicken broth

3 Scotch bonnet chiles, pricked with a fork

¾ cup creamy peanut butter

Cooked white rice for serving

In a large Dutch oven, heat the oil over medium heat. While the oil heats, season the chicken all over with salt and pepper. Add the chicken thighs, skin side down, and the turkey neck to the pot and cook, turning as needed, until browned all over, 5 to 6 minutes. Add the chopped onion and cook, stirring occasionally, until wilted, 3 to 4 minutes. Pour in the water, bring to a simmer, and adjust the heating to maintain a simmer. Cover and cook until the chicken is almost tender, about 20 minutes.

Meanwhile, in a blender, combine the onion chunks, chopped tomatoes, ginger, garlic, tomato paste, paprika, and broth and blend until very smooth.

Uncover the pot, pour in the onion-tomato mixture, and add the chiles. Simmer uncovered, stirring occasionally, until the soup thickens, about 15 minutes.

Scoop out a cup or so of the soup into a medium heatproof bowl and whisk in the peanut butter until smooth. Stir the peanut butter mixture into the pot and continue to simmer the soup until it is thick and flavorful and the chicken is very tender, about 15 minutes more.

To serve, add a scoop of rice to each individual serving bowl, top with a chicken thigh, and then ladle in the soup. Serve hot.

The combination of chicken and shrimp makes this more of a special occasion dish. In Liberia, fish is plentiful because of the country's long Atlantic coastline, so cooks would pair the chicken with whatever seafood is fresh and available. The versatility of this recipe makes it suitable for a wide range of dining occasions, from everyday suppers to elaborate feasts. The dish is prized for its rich flavors and nutritional value, making it a popular choice for both home meals and dining out. Serve this hearty main with rice or plantains.

CHICKEN GRAVY

Spicy Chicken and Tomato Stew

SERVES 6

One 3-pound whole chicken, cut into 10 serving pieces

1 teaspoon seasoning salt

1 teaspoon sweet paprika

½ teaspoon cayenne pepper

¼ cup vegetable oil

½ yellow onion, cut into chunks

1 plum tomato, cut into chunks

¼ cup tomato paste

4 garlic cloves, crushed and peeled

4 cups low-sodium chicken broth

1 Scotch bonnet chile, stemmed and then seeded, if desired

1 red bell pepper, sliced

12 ounces large shrimp, peeled and deveined, with tails intact

Kosher salt

Season the chicken pieces all over with the seasoning salt, paprika, and cayenne. In a large Dutch oven, heat the oil over medium heat. Add the chicken pieces, skin side down, and cook, turning as needed, until browned all over, 8 to 10 minutes.

While the chicken browns, in a blender, combine the onion, tomato, tomato paste, garlic, broth, and chile and blend until very smooth.

Once the chicken is browned, add the onion-tomato mixture, stir well, and bring to a simmer. Adjust the heat to maintain a simmer, cover, and cook until the chicken is almost tender, about 30 minutes.

Uncover, add the bell pepper, and continue to cook uncovered, stirring often, until the sauce is thickened and the bell pepper has softened, about 15 minutes. Stir in the shrimp and simmer until cooked through, about 5 minutes. Taste and season with salt if needed, then serve.

Sweet potato greens are a common vegetable in Liberia. They are usually cooked with mixed boiled meats and/or fried fish, like pompano, but here I provide the simplest preparation. The greens will cook for about an hour total; if you decide to add some protein, you can do this during the last 20 minutes or so of cooking.

RUBBED POTATO GREENS

SERVES 6

2 large bunches sweet potato greens (about 1½ pounds total)

½ teaspoon baking soda

1 yellow onion, cut in chunks

5 garlic cloves, chopped

2 teaspoons chicken bouillon granules

2 Maggi seasoning cubes

⅓ cup red palm or vegetable oil

2 Scotch bonnet chiles, pricked with a fork

Kosher salt

Rinse the greens thoroughly in cold water to rid them of any dirt, then cut off the tough stem bottoms. Tightly grab a bunch of greens in your nondominant fist, holding them tightly around the stems. Using a large, sharp knife in your dominant hand, and working over a large bowl, carefully shave the stems and then the leaves crosswise into the bowl. (This is the traditional way to cut the greens, which creates the classic thin shavings. But if this method makes you nervous, you can finely chop the greens on a cutting board.) Repeat with all of the greens.

Sprinkle the baking soda over the greens and use your hands to mash, squeeze, and rough them up. You want the greens to soften and give up their juices, turning almost into a coarse, dark green pulp. This can take as long as 10 minutes.

In a blender, combine the onion, garlic, bouillon granules, and Maggi cubes and blend until it's a smooth, thick paste.

In a large Dutch oven, heat the oil over medium heat. Add the onion mixture and let sizzle and reduce for a minute or two undisturbed, then add the greens. Cook, stirring often, until the greens begin to give off some liquid, about 10 minutes. Toss in the chiles, cover, and continue to cook, stirring occasionally, until the greens have almost fully dissolved and are thick and deep green, about 1 hour total. Taste and season with salt if needed, then serve.

Quick and easy to make, this rice-based banana bread is a staple in Liberia for breakfast, midday, or a snack. Make sure you purchase cream of rice cereal, *not* cream of wheat. This recipe offers a bonus, too: it is gluten-free.

RICE BREAD

MAKES ONE 8-INCH SQUARE LOAF

½ cup vegetable oil, plus more for the pan

1½ cups cream of rice cereal

⅓ cup sugar

1 teaspoon baking powder

½ teaspoon baking soda

1 teaspoon ground ginger

½ teaspoon salt

¼ teaspoon freshly grated nutmeg

2 large eggs, beaten

¾ cup whole milk

2 very ripe bananas, peeled and mashed

1 teaspoon pure vanilla extract

Preheat the oven to 350°F. Oil the bottom and sides of an 8-inch square baking pan or a 9 by 5-inch loaf pan.

In a large bowl, whisk together the cream of rice cereal, sugar, baking powder, baking soda, ginger, salt, and nutmeg, mixing well. In a medium bowl, whisk together the eggs, milk, oil, bananas, and vanilla until smooth. Pour the egg mixture into the rice cereal mixture and whisk until smooth.

Pour the batter into the prepared baking pan. Bake the bread until golden brown and a toothpick inserted into the center comes out clean, 35 to 40 minutes. Let cool on a wire rack for 15 to 20 minutes before cutting into squares to serve. Serve warm or at room temperature.

This sauce is a staple on Liberian tables, and every recipe is a bit different but it's always extremely spicy. I've added a bell pepper to bulk it up a bit, but don't worry, as it still has an intense amount of heat. If you're new to working with Scotch bonnets, wear gloves and keep a window open when frying the sauce.

FRIED PEPPER SAUCE

MAKES ABOUT 1½ CUPS

1 small yellow onion, cut into chunks

1 red bell pepper, cut into chunks

4 ounces Scotch bonnet chiles (12 to 15), stemmed and then seeded, if desired

6 garlic cloves, crushed and peeled

2 tablespoons distilled white vinegar

1 chicken bouillon cube, crumbled

2 teaspoons kosher salt

¼ cup vegetable oil

In a high-speed blender, combine the onion, bell pepper, chiles, garlic, vinegar, bouillon cube, and salt and blend until very smooth.

In a large saucepan, heat the oil over medium heat. When the oil is hot, carefully add the pepper puree and cook, stirring often, until the sauce is very thick, 10 to 15 minutes. Remove from the heat and let cool before using. The sauce will keep in a tightly capped glass jar or other nonreactive container in the refrigerator for up to 3 weeks.

Also known as puff puff, these sweet fried dough balls are a popular street food in Liberia, similar to a doughnut but with a little more chew. For a truly authentic Liberian flavor, serve with Fried Pepper Sauce (page 230) for dipping.

KALA

Sweet Fried Dough

MAKES ABOUT 12 KALA

2 cups all-purpose flour, plus more if needed

1 packet (2¼ teaspoons) instant dry yeast

⅓ cup sugar, plus more for sprinkling (optional)

½ teaspoon freshly grated nutmeg

½ teaspoon kosher salt

1 cup lukewarm (90° to 100°F) water, plus more if needed

Vegetable oil for frying

In a large bowl, whisk together the flour, yeast, sugar, nutmeg, and salt, mixing well. Add the water and stir with a wooden spoon to make a smooth, loose dough. The dough should be the consistency of thick pancake batter. If it isn't, adjust up or down with a tablespoon or two of water or flour as needed. Cover the bowl with a kitchen towel and let the dough rise in a warm spot until bubbly and almost doubled in size, about 1 hour.

Pour oil to a depth of about 2 inches into a large Dutch oven and heat to 365°F. Line a sheet pan with paper towels and set it near the stove.

When the oil is ready, begin adding the dough, working in two batches to avoid crowding. To make a kala the traditional way, scoop a handful of batter into your palm and squeeze a ball of dough through your palm into the oil. Alternatively, you can drop the dough from a spoon. Fry the dough balls, turning as needed to color evenly, until puffed and golden brown, about 4 minutes. Using a wire skimmer, transfer to the towel-lined sheet pan to drain. Repeat with the remaining dough, always allowing the oil to return to 365°F before adding the second batch.

Sprinkle the balls with sugar, if desired, and serve hot.

This two-ingredient sweet is similar to dulce de leche but thicker and chewier. If you have sesame seeds on hand, they make a nice, crunchy topping. But a pinch of chopped nuts or even a single almond or peanut on each candy would also be delicious.

MILK CANDY

MAKES ABOUT 18 PIECES

2 tablespoons vegetable oil, plus more for brushing and your hands

One 14-ounce can sweetened condensed milk

Toasted sesame seeds or chopped nuts, for garnish, if desired

Brush a nonstick sheet pan with oil.

In a small, heavy saucepan, heat the oil over medium-low heat. When the oil is hot, add the condensed milk, bring to a simmer, and cook, stirring constantly, until the milk is very thick and has darkened several shades—slightly darker than peanut butter. This can take 15 minutes or more, so you will need to be patient!

Pour onto the prepared sheet pan and let cool just until you can touch it. (Keep it as hot as you can comfortably touch so it will be easier to shape.) To shape each candy, oil your hands, pinch off a scant tablespoon-size piece of the mixture, roll into a ball, and place back on the sheet pan. Press your thumb in the center of each ball to make a small depression and to flatten the ball slightly.

If desired, sprinkle some sesame seeds in each depression. Let the candies cool completely, then place each candy in a paper candy cup for serving. The candies will keep in an airtight container at room temperature for 3 to 4 days.

YEMEN

LEARN HOW TO PRONOUNCE
THE RECIPE NAME

YEMEN

Yemen was one of the four countries I was unable to visit personally. I knew I needed help on the ground, so I reached out to acclaimed coffee roaster and friend Moktar Alkhanshali. He was able to introduce me to Somaya Samawi, a talented Yemeni photographer known for her enthralling images of Yemen's landscapes, people, and culture. In her work, Somaya beautifully and intimately captured the essence of her cherished homeland, infusing each photo in this chapter with a profound sense of wonder and care.

BACKGROUND

Yemen, officially known as the Republic of Yemen, is located on the Arabian Peninsula in western Asia. It is bordered by Saudi Arabia to the north, Oman to the east, and the Red Sea and the Arabian Sea to the west and south, respectively. Yemen is one of the oldest centers of civilization and has a rich historical and cultural heritage.

Yemen covers an area of approximately 528,000 square kilometers (203,862 square miles) and has a population of over 35 million in 2024. Arabic is the official language, and Islam is the predominant religion. The country's capital and largest city is Sana'a, renowned for its distinctive architecture characterized by ancient multistory mud-brick buildings adorned with intricate geometric patterns.

Yemen has a diverse ethnic and tribal composition, with Arab groups forming the majority. A long history of tribal affiliations and regional divisions has influenced the political landscape. Yemen has faced challenges in establishing stable governance structures and has experienced periods of political unrest and armed conflicts.

Historically, Yemen was divided into two separate entities: North Yemen and South Yemen. North Yemen gained independence from the Ottoman Empire in 1918, while South Yemen achieved independence from British colonial rule in 1967. The two countries unified in 1990 to form the Republic of Yemen.

2024

Yemen has faced significant challenges, including political instability, armed conflicts, and a severed humanitarian crisis. The ongoing conflict between the internationally recognized government and the Houthi rebels has resulted in widespread devastation, including civilian casualties and displacement. The conflict has also allowed extremist groups, like Al-Qaeda in the Arabian Peninsula (AQAP), to gain footholds in certain areas.

Yemen's infrastructure has been heavily damaged, and access to basic services, such as health care, clean water, and education, has been severely limited. The country is highly dependent on humanitarian aid from international organizations to meet the needs of its population.

Efforts to find a peaceful resolution to the conflict and restore stability in Yemen continue, but progress has been slow and challenging. International diplomatic initiatives, humanitarian assistance, and support for Yemen's reconstruction are crucial to alleviating the suffering of the Yemeni people.

MOKHTAR ALKHANSHALI

Mokhtar Alkhanshali's background spans Brooklyn, San Francisco, and Yemen. His familial roots extend deep into Yemen's agricultural history, where his ancestors have cultivated coffee for generations.

Initially, Mokhtar devoted himself to community organizing in San Francisco, championing civil rights causes for Arab, Muslim, and immigrant communities. However, a pivotal moment led him to rekindle his family's ties to coffee farming.

Motivated to revitalize Yemen's struggling coffee industry, Mokhtar embarked on establishing Port of Mokha, through which he hoped to import coffee from Yemen. His objective? To rejuvenate Yemeni coffee production. Through his expertise in specialty coffee production and innovative strategies, he successfully revitalized Yemeni coffee, reclaiming its position as a coveted commodity. Mokhtar's efforts achieved global recognition in 2017 when his coffee earned the top ranking by the prestigious industry publication *Coffee Review*.

In 2020, Mokhtar collaborated with coffee expert Willem Boot to establish the Mokha Institute, a nonprofit organization committed to leveraging coffee for social and economic advancement in Yemen. The mission of the institute is to aid Yemen's recovery from the devastation of war by utilizing coffee to foster employment opportunities and community empowerment.

Mokhtar's journey embodies resilience, dedication, and a profound commitment to the world of coffee. And rest assured, his story is far from reaching its conclusion.

Made with the husks of coffee beans (not the beans themselves), this traditional Yemeni drink is almost like a cross between a coffee and a tea. It's spiced with ginger, which aids in digestion, making it a perfect morning drink or a light after-dinner offering. Coffee husks can be purchased from health food stores or online. You can also buy them from some coffee roasters, as they are a by-product of roasting. Here, I use a pot and a fine-mesh sieve for making the drink, but a French press coffee maker works well too.

QISHR

Ginger Coffee Husk Drink

SERVES 3 TO 4

1 cup coffee husks

3 cups water

1-inch piece fresh ginger, grated

2 tablespoons sugar, plus more for serving

¼ teaspoon ground cinnamon

Working in batches if needed, grind the coffee husks in a spice grinder until very coarsely ground.

In a medium saucepan, bring the water to a rolling boil over high heat. Add the ground husks, ginger, sugar, and cinnamon, remove from the heat, and cover the pot. Let steep for 8 minutes, stirring and re-covering halfway through.

Strain the drink through a fine-mesh sieve into cups and serve hot, passing sugar at the table for adding to taste.

Shakshouka is a common dish in the Middle East and North Africa, where the eggs are typically poached in the thick tomato sauce. In Yemen, in contrast, the eggs are lightly scrambled with the sauce.

Despite this dish coming together in just minutes, it is rich and flavorful and makes a great breakfast or light supper with the fried flatbread (see page 257) and a drizzle of Sahawiq | Spicy Cilantro Condiment (page 261).

SHAKSHOUKA

Spiced Scrambled Eggs

SERVES 4

3 tablespoons extra-virgin olive oil

1 small yellow onion, finely chopped

4 plum tomatoes, chopped

1 jalapeño chile, seeded, if desired, and finely chopped

Kosher salt

6 large eggs

1 tablespoon tomato paste

3 garlic cloves, finely chopped

2 teaspoons Hawaij | Yemeni Spice Blend (page 262)

2 tablespoons chopped fresh flat-leaf parsley leaves

In a large nonstick skillet, heat the oil over medium heat. When the oil is hot, add the onion and cook, stirring occasionally, until softened, about 5 minutes. Add the chopped tomatoes, chile, and 1 teaspoon salt and cook, stirring occasionally, until the tomatoes give up their juices, about 5 minutes. Increase the heat to medium-high to reduce the juices and thicken the mixture, 3 to 4 minutes more.

While the tomatoes cook, in a medium bowl, whisk together the eggs and ½ teaspoon salt until blended. When the tomatoes have thickened, add the tomato paste, garlic, and hawaij to the skillet and cook and stir until sizzling, about 1 minute. Pour the eggs into the skillet and stir just until the eggs are softly set, 3 to 4 minutes.

Remove the skillet from the heat and let rest for a few minutes to finish cooking the eggs to your liking. Garnish with parsley and serve immediately, with warm flatbread if you like.

This quick and economical dish, made even faster with canned favas, is on the table from breakfast to dinner in Yemen and is often served in a heated clay pot to keep it piping hot throughout the meal. The consistency should fall somewhere between a soup and a stew. Serve this classic Yemeni comfort food with Malawach | Flaky Fried Flatbread (page 257) or another flatbread for scooping.

FOUL MOUDAMMAS

Fava Bean Stew

SERVES 4

3 tablespoons extra-virgin olive oil, plus more for drizzling

1 small yellow onion, finely chopped

2 plum tomatoes, chopped

1 small jalapeño chile, seeded, if desired, and chopped, plus more for garnish

2 garlic cloves, finely chopped

Kosher salt

1 teaspoon ground coriander

1 teaspoon ground cumin

Two 15½-ounce cans fava beans, drained and rinsed

2 cups water

Chopped fresh cilantro for garnish

In a medium Dutch oven, heat the oil over medium heat. Add the onion and cook, stirring occasionally, until wilted and golden, 7 to 8 minutes. Add the tomatoes, chile, and garlic, season with salt, and cook, stirring often, until the tomatoes release their juices, the juices evaporate, and a thick, chunky paste remains in the bottom of the pot, 6 to 8 minutes.

Add the coriander and cumin and stir to incorporate into the tomato mixture. Add the favas and water, bring to a simmer, and cook until the favas are very tender and beginning to fall apart, about 15 minutes. Mash with a potato masher or the back of a wooden spoon until the mixture is creamy but still a bit chunky, adding a little more water if it seems too thick. Taste and adjust the seasoning with salt if needed.

Spoon the stew into a serving dish. Top with a drizzle of oil, garnish with chile and cilantro, and serve hot.

Traditionally cooked and served in a stone pot, this comforting stew, considered by many the national dish of Yemen, can be made with or without meat, substituting whatever vegetables you have on hand for the lamb. Red bell peppers, okra, tomatoes, and/or more potatoes would all be good choices. Hulba, the finishing condiment, is finely ground fenugreek that expands and lightens when mixed with water and whips up to a frothy foam. A popular condiment in Yemen, it adds a tangy, slightly bitter flavor to stews and soups.

SALTAH

Lamb Stew with Fenugreek Froth

SERVES 4 TO 6

STEW

1½ pounds boneless lamb shoulder, cut into cubes

1 teaspoon ground cumin

1 teaspoon ground coriander

½ teaspoon ground turmeric

Kosher salt and freshly ground black pepper

2 tablespoons extra-virgin olive oil

1 small yellow onion, chopped

1 small green bell pepper, chopped

2 plum tomatoes, chopped

1 small jalapeño chile, chopped (if desired, remove seeds for less heat)

2 garlic cloves, chopped

2 cups low-sodium beef broth

2 cups water

2 russet potatoes, peeled and cut into large chunks

To make the stew: Put the lamb into a medium bowl and sprinkle with the cumin, coriander, turmeric, 1 teaspoon salt, and a few generous grinds of pepper. Toss to coat the lamb in the seasonings.

In a large Dutch oven, heat the oil over medium heat. Add the lamb and cook, turning as needed, until browned all over, 5 to 6 minutes. Add the onion, bell pepper, tomato, and chile, stir well, and cook, stirring occasionally, until the vegetables begin to wilt, about 5 minutes. Add the garlic and cook, stirring, until fragrant, about 1 minute. Pour in the broth and water, bring to a simmer, adjust the heat to maintain a simmer, cover, and cook until the lamb is just beginning to become tender, about 40 minutes.

Uncover and add the potatoes. Re-cover and continue to simmer until the lamb is very tender and the potatoes are cooked, 30 to 40 minutes more.

Uncover and use a fork or wooden spoon to break apart and mash the lamb slightly. The consistency should be that of a thick soup or thin stew, so reduce slightly over medium heat if needed.

CONTINUED

SALTAH

CONTINUED

HULBA

2 tablespoons ground fenugreek

2 cups water

Juice of ½ lemon

1 tablespoon Sahawiq | Spicy Cilantro Condiment (page 261)

Kosher salt

Once the stew is cooking, make the hulba: In a medium bowl, combine the fenugreek and water. Stir and then let soak until the fenugreek has absorbed some of the water and become a paste, about 1 hour. Drain off all but about 1 tablespoon of the water. Transfer the paste and reserved water to a larger bowl, add the lemon juice, and beat together with an electric mixer on high speed until light and foamy, about 2 minutes. If the mixture is still thick and flat, add a tablespoon or two of water and continue to beat on high speed until foamy. Add the sahawiq and whisk until smooth. Season with salt.

Ladle the stew into individual bowls and top with spoonfuls of the hulba. Serve hot.

These thick, round flatbreads pull apart in buttery, flaky layers, so they are best served hot from the griddle. They're a bit of a project to make, so in Yemen you'll find them more often in restaurants than in homes. They are commonly enjoyed as a breakfast or brunch dish. They can be served plain with savory toppings such as grated tomato and hard-boiled eggs. They're also sometimes enjoyed with sweet toppings like honey and jam.

MALAWACH

Flaky Fried Flatbread

MAKES FOUR 8-INCH FLATBREADS

2 cups bread flour, plus more for the work surface

1 teaspoon kosher salt

5 tablespoons ghee or unsalted butter, melted and cooled, plus 2 to 3 tablespoons melted for brushing

¾ cup water, at room temperature, plus more if needed

In a large bowl, stir together the flour and salt. Drizzle the ghee evenly over the flour mixture and toss with a fork to coat the flour with the fat. Pour in the water and toss until an evenly moistened, crumbly dough forms. Using your hands, mix the dough in the bowl just until it comes together in a ball, adding more water, a little at a time (up to ¼ cup total), if the dough is still too crumbly.

Transfer the dough to a lightly floured work surface and knead until very soft and smooth, 5 to 7 minutes. Form into a ball, brush on all sides with a little melted ghee, and wrap the ball in plastic wrap. Let rest on the work surface for 30 minutes.

Line a sheet pan with parchment paper. Remove the plastic wrap and divide the dough into four equal pieces. Place one piece on a clean work surface, keeping the remaining pieces lightly covered with the plastic wrap. Stretch and roll the piece into a very thin rectangle about 12 by 8 inches. (You shouldn't need flour to roll at this point.) Brush the top surface of the rectangle with ghee. Starting from the long side nearest you, fold the rectangle up into a flat strip about 1 inch wide. Spiral the dough strip into a tight coil and lay the coil on the prepared sheet pan. Repeat with the remaining three dough pieces. Cover the sheet pan with a kitchen towel and let the dough rest for another 30 minutes.

CONTINUED

MALAWACH

CONTINUED

On a clean work surface, using a rolling pin, roll each coil into an 8-inch round flatbread. Heat a large cast-iron skillet or griddle over medium-high heat. When the pan is hot, add as many flatbreads as will fit comfortably and cook until charred on the underside, 2 to 3 minutes. Flip and cook the second side in the same manner, 2 to 3 minutes more. Repeat with the remaining flatbreads. Serve hot.

This all-purpose Yemeni sauce is traditionally made in a mortar and pestle. Lacking that setup, you can grind the spice seeds in a spice grinder, then pulse them with the remaining ingredients in a food processor.

To make this sauce up to 8 hours ahead of serving, add all the ingredients up to the lemon juice, then work in the lemon juice just before serving so the herbs don't discolor. The sauce is great on fried foods, such as falafel, fish, vegetables, and grilled meats.

SAHAWIQ

Spicy Cilantro Condiment

MAKES ABOUT 1½ CUPS

2 teaspoons coriander seeds

1 teaspoon cumin seeds

Seeds from 6 green cardamom pods (about 60 seeds)

4 garlic cloves, crushed and peeled

2 jalapeño chiles, chopped

Leaves and tender stems from 1 small bunch cilantro (about 2 cups)

1 cup loosely packed fresh flat-leaf parsley leaves

Kosher salt

½ cup extra-virgin olive oil

Juice of ½ lemon

In a small skillet, combine the coriander, cumin, and cardamom seeds over low heat and toast, stirring constantly, until fragrant, 1 to 2 minutes. Pour into a small bowl and let cool completely.

Transfer the cooled spices to a mortar and work with a pestle until finely ground. Add the garlic and chiles and work with the pestle to make a thick paste. Add as much cilantro and parsley as will fit in the mortar and work with the pestle until ground to a paste. Continue adding the herbs as you grind until all are reduced to a paste.

Once all of the herbs are ground, mix in 1 teaspoon salt. Drizzle in the oil, a little at a time, working the pestle in a circular motion to incorporate the oil as you go. Once all of the oil has been incorporated, work in the lemon juice. Let the sauce sit for 15 minutes to allow the flavors to develop before serving.

There are two types of hawaij in Yemen, one used for savory preparations and one used for sweeter ones, such as for baking or in coffee or tea. Countless variations of both versions exist, with many home cooks and restaurant chefs having their own blend. This recipe is a savory mix, and you'll find lots of uses for it in your kitchen, from soups and stews to roasted meats and vegetables.

HAWAIJ

Yemeni Spice Blend

MAKES ABOUT ¾ CUP

⅓ cup black peppercorns

¼ cup cumin seeds

2 tablespoons coriander seeds

2 tablespoons green cardamom pods

1 teaspoon whole cloves

3 tablespoons ground turmeric

In a small skillet, combine the peppercorns, cumin, coriander, cardamom, and cloves and toast over medium-low heat, shaking the pan almost constantly to prevent scorching, until a few seeds begin to pop and the mixture is very fragrant, about 2 minutes. Pour into a small bowl and let cool completely.

Transfer the cooled spices to a spice grinder and pulse to a fine powder. If there are still some lumps, sift the ground spices through a fine-mesh sieve, return the chunks to the grinder, and pulse again. Once all the spices are ground, stir in the turmeric. Transfer to an airtight container and store in the pantry for up to several months or in the freezer for up to 2 months.

This version of aseeda is the sweet iteration of the thick, boiled wheat dish, a staple of the Yemeni diet. It can be eaten for breakfast or as a dessert or snack and can be topped with dried fruit. There's also a savory version, typically finished with a rich lamb broth. Either way, this dish requires a lot of elbow grease and is meant to be shared communally, scooped up with the fingers.

ASEEDA

Boiled Wheat Pudding

SERVES 6

2½ cups all-purpose flour

3 cups water

1 teaspoon kosher salt

2 tablespoons unsalted butter, cubed, plus 3 tablespoons melted

Honey or date syrup for drizzling

Sift the flour into a medium bowl and set aside. In a medium saucepan (large enough to hold the flour), combine 2 cups of the water, the salt, and the 2 tablespoons cubed butter and bring to a boil over high heat. Remove from the heat and whisk in the flour, mixing well. Switch to a wooden spoon and stir (still off the heat) until the mixture is smooth, completely free of lumps, and no longer sticky (this will take some work!), 3 to 4 minutes. It will be a thick paste.

Add the remaining 1 cup water and return the pan to very low heat. Using the wooden spoon, break up the flour mixture into small pieces and then stir to make a cohesive mass once again. Continue to cook and stir until the mixture is very thick and completely dried out, 5 to 6 minutes.

Liberally brush a large serving plate with about 1 tablespoon of the melted butter. Transfer the flour mixture to the plate and fold it over onto itself to make a smooth mound. Make a depression in the center and fill with the remaining 2 tablespoons melted butter. Drizzle a little honey in the depression and then drizzle more around the edges. Set the platter in the center of the table and serve hot.

Masoub, also known as Masoob or Malikia, is a traditional dish renowned in Yemen and throughout the Arabian Peninsula. It is characterized by its simplicity, with basic yet flavorful ingredients such as ripe bananas, bread, and cream. While Yemen takes pride in its association with this dish, variations of it can be found in other regions such as Saudi Arabia, Oman, and Somalia. This dish is a genius use of day-old bread and of bananas that are past their prime, coming together in just a few minutes. It can be enjoyed as either a dessert or a breakfast dish.

MASOUB

Banana and Flatbread Pudding

SERVES 4 TO 6

2 day-old 6-inch flatbreads (such as pita, paratha, naan, or khubz, page 165)

4 very ripe bananas, peeled

½ cup cold heavy cream

3 tablespoons honey

½ cup pitted dates, chopped

¼ cup raisins

¼ cup sliced almonds, toasted

Tear the flatbreads into rough chunks, drop into a food processor, and pulse to coarse crumbs (be careful not to overprocess or you will end up with paste). You should have about 2 heaping cups.

Transfer the crumbs to a medium skillet and toast over medium heat, stirring often, until lightly toasted, 2 to 4 minutes. Remove from the heat.

In a large bowl, mash the bananas with a fork until chunky. Add the toasted crumbs and stir until well mixed and a thick paste forms. Let sit for a few minutes to thicken further while you whip the cream and ready the garnishes.

In a medium bowl, whisk the cream just until it begins to hold peaks but can still be drizzled.

Mound the bread-banana mixture in a shallow serving bowl and smooth into an even shape. Drizzle with the cream and honey and sprinkle with the dates, raisins, and almonds.

90,000 years ago

● **Yemen 90,000 years ago**—Central African foragers inhabit the region that is now Yemen.

3100 BCE

● **Egypt c. 3100 BCE**—Ancient Egypt's first dynasty emerges, marking the beginning of pharaonic rule.

300 BCE

● **Egypt 332 BCE**—Alexander the Great conquers Egypt.

● **Egypt 305 BCE**—The Ptolemaic Kingdom is established.

1500s

● **Yemen 1500–1899**—Other kingdoms, including the Kingdom of Hadhramaut and the Kathiri Sultanate, have influence in Yemen.

● **Egypt 1517**—Egypt becomes part of the Ottoman Empire.

1600s–1750s

● **Democratic Republic of Congo 1665–1709**—Kongo Civil War.

● **Afghanistan 1747**—Ahmad Shah Durrani establishes the modern state of Afghanistan.

1800s

● **Egypt 1805**—Muhammad Ali Pasha comes to power, initiating a series of reforms and modernization efforts.

● **El Salvador 1821**—El Salvador gains independence from Spain, and eventually becomes part of the United Provinces of Central America in 1823.

● **Liberia 1822**—The American Colonization Society establishes a settlement on the land that would become known as Liberia for freed African American slaves.

● **Liberia 1847**—Liberia declares independence and becomes the first independent republic in Africa.

KEY

● Afghanistan
● Democratic Republic of Congo
● Egypt
● El Salvador
● Iraq
● Lebanon
● Liberia
● Yemen

TIMELIN

30 BCE

● **Egypt 30 BCE**—Egypt becomes a province of the Roman Empire following the death of Cleopatra.

600 CE

● **Egypt 641 CE**—Arab Muslim armies invade Egypt, marking the beginning of Arab rule.

1300s

● **Yemen 1300–1899**—The Kingdom of Yemen, also known as the Kingdom of Saba, flourishes in the region.

● **Yemen 1870s**—European exploration of Yemen begins, with figures like Sir Richard Burton and Heinrich Barth visiting the region.

● **Egypt 1882**—British forces occupy Egypt, leading to a period of British colonial rule.

1900–1950s

● **Yemen 1918**—North Yemen gains independence from the Ottoman Empire.

● **Egypt 1922**—Egypt gains independence from Britain but remains under British political influence.

● **El Salvador 1932**—The Salvadoran peasant revolt and subsequent massacre, known as La Matanza, results in a brutal government crackdown, leading to significant political repression.

● **Iraq 1932**—Iraq gains independence from British control.

● **Lebanon 1943**—Lebanon gains independence from the League of Nations mandate under French administration.

1950–1970s

● **Egypt 1952**—The Egyptian Revolution takes place, leading to the overthrow of the monarchy and the establishment of a republic.

● **Iraq 1958**—Revolution leads to the overthrow of the monarchy and the establishment of a republican government.

● **Democratic Republic of Congo 1960–65**—Congo Crisis (dating from the country's independence from Belgium to the rise of dictator Mobutu Sese Seko).

● **Yemen 1967**—South Yemen achieves independence from British colonial rule.

1970s

● **El Salvador 1970s**—Growing social and economic inequalities contribute to widespread discontent and political unrest.

● **Lebanon 1975–90**—Lebanese Civil War, involving various factions and foreign interventions.

● **Egypt 1979**—Egypt signs a peace treaty with Israel, becoming the first Arab country to do so.

● **El Salvador 1979**—A military coup takes place, leading to the establishment of a military junta.

● **Afghanistan 1979–89**—Soviet-Afghan War.

1980s

● **El Salvador 1980**—Archbishop Óscar Romero is assassinated, escalating tensions and drawing international attention to the human rights abuses in the country.

● **Liberia 1980**—A military coup led by Samuel Doe overthrows the government, leading to a period of political instability and human rights abuses.

● **El Salvador 1980–92**—Salvadoran Civil War ensues, characterized by intense conflict between government forces and leftist guerrilla groups, notably the Farabundo Martí National Liberation Front (FMLN). The conflict sees widespread human rights abuses, including massacres and disappearances.

● **Iraq 1980–88**—Iran-Iraq War, resulting in massive casualties and economic damage.

● **El Salvador 1981–92**—The United States provides significant military and financial support to the Salvadoran government in its fight against the FMLN, contributing to the complexity of the conflict.

● **Lebanon 1982**—Israel invades Lebanon to remove the Palestine Liberation Organization (PLO) forces.

● **Afghanistan 1989–96**—Period of civil war and political instability.

● **Liberia 1989–97**—The First Liberian Civil War erupts, characterized by fighting between various rebel groups, government forces, and regional factions. The conflict results in widespread devastation and loss of life.

1990s

● **Democratic Republic of Congo 1996–97**—First Republic of the Congo Civil War (led to the overthrow of Mobutu by Laurent-Désiré Kabila and his rebel forces).

● **Afghanistan 1996–2001**—Taliban regime controls a significant portion of Afghanistan.

● **Democratic Republic of Congo May 1997**—Mobutu flees into exile. With minimal resistance, the Alliance for Democratic Liberation (AFDL) and the Rwandan army seize Kinshasa, and rebel leader Laurent-Désiré Kabila becomes president. The name of the country is changed from Zaire to the Democratic Republic of Congo.

● **Liberia 1997**—Charles Taylor, a former warlord, is elected president of Liberia.

● **Democratic Republic of Congo 1997–2003**—Second Republic of the Congo Civil War (involved nine nations and led to ongoing low-level warfare despite an official peace treaty).

● **Democratic Republic of Congo 1999–2003**—Ituri Conflict (sub-conflict of the Second Republic of the Congo Civil War. The Movement for the Liberation of the Congo committed genocide on the Mbuti and other Pygmy tribes in North Kivu).

● **Liberia 1999–2003**—The Second Liberian Civil War takes place, with rebel groups fighting against the government forces led by Charles Taylor. The war leads to further destruction and displacement of the population.

1990s

● **Yemen 1990**—North Yemen and South Yemen merge to form the Republic of Yemen.

● **Iraq 1990–91**—Iraq invades Kuwait, leading to the Gulf War and subsequent international intervention.

● **El Salvador 1992**—The Chapultepec Peace Accords are signed, officially ending the civil war. The FMLN transforms into a political party, and efforts begin to establish a more inclusive and democratic government.

● **El Salvador 1994**—The FMLN participates in the first postwar elections, marking a shift toward a more peaceful political process.

● **Yemen 1994**—Civil war breaks out between forces loyal to the former South Yemen—the People's Democratic Republic of Yemen (PDRY), which existed as a separate state from North Yemen until the unification of Yemen in 1990—and those loyal to the unified government. The conflict results in the victory of the government forces and the consolidation of power.

● **Democratic Republic of Congo April 1994**—When Tutsi rebels took control of Rwanda during the Rwandan Civil War, over a million Hutus took refuge in camps in Zaire. It's estimated that fifty thousand people died in the first month when cholera spread through the squalid refugee camps in eastern Zaire.

● **Democratic Republic of Congo November 1994**—Aid agencies stopped working in refugee camps, stating that they had become increasingly militarized by former Rwandan Hutu soldiers controlling access to food distribution.

● **Democratic Republic of Congo October 1996**—The Rwandan army, in support of an anti-Mobutu rebel group, attacks refugee camps in eastern Zaire and marches on the capital, Kinshasa. Tens of thousands of Rwandan Hutu refugees flee westward into Zaire's forests pursued by Rwandan army soldiers.

2000s

● **Afghanistan 2001**—US-led coalition invades and over-throws the Taliban regime.

● **Afghanistan 2001–present**—Efforts to establish a democratic government and rebuild infrastructure.

● **Iraq 2003**—Coalition forces led by the United States invade Iraq, overthrowing the government of Saddam Hussein.

● **Liberia 2003**—Charles Taylor is forced into exile, and a transitional government is established.

● **Yemen 2004**—Houthi insurgency begins in the north of Yemen, led by the Houthi movement.

● **Lebanon 2005**—The Cedar Revolution takes place after the assassination of former Prime Minister Rafik Hariri, leading to the withdrawal of Syrian forces from Lebanon.

● **Liberia 2005**—Ellen Johnson Sirleaf becomes the first female elected head of state in Africa, marking a turning point for Liberia.

● **Lebanon 2006**—Israel and Hezbollah engage in a conflict in southern Lebanon.

● **Iraq 2006–2007**—Sectarian violence escalates in Iraq, leading to a surge in US military presence and efforts to stabilize the country.

● **El Salvador 2009**—Mauricio Funes, a former journalist and member of the FMLN, is elected president of El Salvador, signaling a historic victory for the former guerrilla group in the political arena.

2010s

● **Egypt 2011**—The Egyptian Revolution begins, leading to the ousting of President Hosni Mubarak.

● **Lebanon 2011**—The Syrian Civil War begins, impacting Lebanon due to the influx of refugees and spillover violence.

● **Liberia 2011**—Ellen Johnson Sirleaf is reelected for a second term as president.

● **Yemen 2011**—Yemen experiences widespread protests as part of the Arab Spring movement. President Ali Abdullah Saleh resigns, and a transitional government is formed.

● **Egypt 2012**—Mohamed Morsi becomes Egypt's first democratically elected president.

● **Egypt 2013**—Following mass protests, Mohamed Morsi is overthrown by the military, and Abdul Fattah al-Sisi assumes power.

● **Afghanistan 2014**—Withdrawal of most NATO combat troops from Afghanistan.

● **El Salvador 2014**—Gang violence and economic challenges contribute to a rise in social unrest, leading to concerns about the country's stability.

● **Yemen 2014**—Houthi rebels seize control of the capital, Sana'a, and large parts of the country.

● **Yemen 2015**—President Abdrabbuh Mansur Hadi flees to Saudi Arabia.

● **Democratic Republic of Congo 2019**—Following a disputed general election in 2018, Félix Tshisekedi becomes president, a position he holds at the time of writing.

● **Iraq 2014–17**—The Islamic State (IS) captures significant territory in Iraq, leading to a major military campaign to reclaim lost areas.

2021

● **Afghanistan 2021**—US announces the withdrawal of troops is complete, leading to increased instability and the resurgence of the Taliban.

● **Egypt 2021**—Egypt continues to navigate political, economic, and social challenges while striving for stability and development.

● **El Salvador 2021**—President Nayib Bukele consolidates power, raising concerns about democratic institutions and governance. International scrutiny increases as Bukele's administration faces accusations of authoritarianism.

● **Iraq 2021**—Iraq faces ongoing security challenges, including sporadic attacks by extremist groups and tensions in the region.

2023

● **Liberia 2023**—Liberia continues to work toward stability, economic growth, and social development, addressing challenges such as corruption, poverty, and infrastructure development.

2024

● **El Salvador 2024**—Ongoing efforts to address economic issues, social inequality, and political challenges continue, with the international community closely monitoring the situation.

2020

● **Yemen 2015–present**—Saudi Arabia leads a military intervention in Yemen to support the internationally recognized government and counter the Houthi rebels. The conflict leads to a humanitarian crisis, with widespread civilian casualties and displacement.

● **Liberia 2017**—George Weah, a former professional football player, is elected president of Liberia.

● **Iraq 2018**—Iraq holds parliamentary elections, and a new government is formed.

● **El Salvador 2019**—Nayib Bukele, a former mayor of San Salvador, wins the presidential election, representing a departure from the traditional political parties.

● **Iraq 2019–20**—Widespread protests erupt across Iraq, demanding political reforms, improved services, and an end to corruption.

● **Lebanon 2019–20**—Widespread protests erupt across Lebanon against government corruption and economic mismanagement.

● **Lebanon 2020**—Economic crisis worsens, leading to a depreciation of the Lebanese currency and protests demanding political and economic reforms.

● **Lebanon 2020**—Lebanon faces a devastating explosion at the port of Beirut due to a large quantity of ammonium nitrate improperly stored at a warehouse. The explosion, one of the most powerful nonnuclear explosions in history, results in significant loss of life and sweeping destruction.

● **Yemen 2020**—Ongoing peace talks and diplomatic efforts aim to find a resolution to the Yemeni conflict.

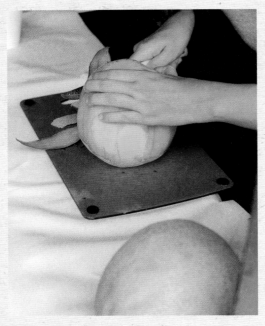

RESOURCES

Afghanistan: moci.gov.af/en

Democratic Republic of Congo: ambadrcusa.org

Egypt: egypt.travel

El Salvador: elsalvador.travel/en

Iraq: mofa.gov.iq/en

Lebanon: visit-lebanon.org/leisure

Liberia: enjoyliberia.travel

Yemen: mot.gov.ye/?lang=en

ACKNOWLEDGMENTS

It takes a village to accomplish most things, including writing a book. I am deeply grateful to everyone who welcomed me into their homes, shared their stories, cooked for me, and offered their time and space. Creativity is all about connecting dots, and many thanks are due to the following people and organizations who made this book possible:

In Afghanistan: Stephanie Mahmoud, Ali Zaman, Ziba Food (check them out at @zibafoods), and photographers Omer Khan, Mahab Azizi, and Belal Mostamand.

In Democratic Republic of Congo: Kaniaru Wacieni, Lena Militsi, John Kanyoni, and the kids Stephane, Ntare, and Neza—thank you for having me over for dinner and allowing me to occupy so much of your parents' time. Special thanks also to Nathalie Kala Konga, the staff at Ubuntu Restaurant, Chef Christian Yumbi, Elayla (Emily) Ndelela, Sakha Gueye, and Amini Kajunju, who is not only my Congolese sister but also the cultural editor for this book. Your help was invaluable.

In Egypt: Rana Abdelhamid, my dear friend, and the talented photographer Doaa Elkady, who not only modeled for the food photos but also traveled extensively across Egypt to gather the beautiful images for this book. Your contributions are deeply appreciated.

In El Salvador: Camilo Menéndez, Palo Verde Sustainable Hotel, our guide and fixer Luis Rodrigo Rivas of El Zonte Tours, and Francisco and Maria Martinez.

In Iraq: Ayad Asha and Aline Deschamps, who captured this chapter through their lens while traveling in Iraq. Your vision, kindness, and friendship have been crucial to this book.

In Lebanon: Omar Abboud, Rami Abou-Khalil, Kamal Mouzawak, Elie Obeid, the folks at Souk El Tayeb, Muneeb Hyder, Mikey Muhanna, and everyone at Egan Legna (check them out @egnalegna) who generously shared their stories and time. Thank you also to Salah Nader. Your support and insights about Lebanon have been a huge help and have really deepened my understanding of the region.

In Liberia: Tanya Ansahta Garnett, Talahta Murcy, Ahsatu Murcy, Nya S. Gbaintor, Esq., and Paul Donnieh.

In Yemen: Mokhtar Alkhanshal (check out @portofmokha for coffee by Mokhtar) and Somaya Samawi for capturing the stunning photos in this chapter.

A special thank-you to Sabine Mondesir for your help in the kitchen during our food shoot days. Your assistance ensured everything ran smoothly. Amy

Stevenson, my dear friend and longtime collaborator, thank you for your unwavering trust in the process, your organizational skills, and your contribution to the recipe development. I'm so grateful for you.

Riley Dengler, thank you for traveling near and far with me to capture this book so beautifully. I couldn't have asked for a better teammate and friend to navigate the unknown with. Julie Gartland, thank you for spending four magical days at Shio Studio (check them out at @shiostudio) in Brooklyn and for adding so much beauty to this book with your photos. And to Daniel, thank you for being such a fantastic photo assistant to Julia.

Alya Hameedi, thank you for stepping in at the last minute to style our food shoots and for bringing such calm to the set. Thanks also to everyone at Ten Speed for supporting my wild ideas and for your endless encouragement.

Thank you to my wonderful editors, Dervla Kelly and Claire Yee, who always see the big picture while helping me focus on the tiny details. I'm so grateful for your expertise and understanding, as well as Isabelle Gioffredi, Emma Campion, and Brianne Sperber.

To my dear friend, agent, and collaborator Kari, thank you for believing in my work and in a world beyond just you and me. I am truly grateful for you, for our walks, and for everything in between.

To my hooyo, thank you for this life and for my siblings. To my besties, Noelle Bonner, Kojo Yeboah, and Nuno Santo, and to my auntie-bestie, Sheila Cochran, thank you for your unwavering support.

I would like to express my gratitude to a few products featured in the book. Thank you to Jefferson Ellison, Connie Matisse, and the crew at East Fork for the beautiful pottery showcased in the book (find them on Instagram @eastforkpottery). I am also very grateful to Staub Cookware for the stunning cookware featured throughout.

ABOUT THE AUTHOR

Photo copyright © Riley Dengler

Hawa Hassan is host of Food Network's *Hawa at Home* and Cooking Channel's *Spice of Life*, acclaimed author of James Beard Award–winning *In Bibi's Kitchen*, and founder and CEO of Basbaas, makers of African-inspired sauces and condiments. An acclaimed speaker and presenter, Hawa has been covered by major international media including *The New York Times, Vogue, Vanity Fair, The Wall Street Journal, Bon Appétit, The Seattle Times, Condé Nast Traveler*, Thrillist, *Ebony*, The Ringer, *San Francisco Chronicle, Forbes, The Washington Post,* and *New York Magazine.*

INDEX

Published in the United States by Ten Speed Press,
an imprint of the Crown Publishing Group, a division
of Penguin Random House LLC, New York.
TenSpeed.com

Ten Speed Press and the Ten Speed Press colophon are
registered trademarks of Penguin Random House LLC.

Typefaces: Dinamo's ABC Arizona Flare, Hoefler&Co.'s
Gotham, and Art Grootfontein's Bangel

Penguin Random House collects and processes your
personal information. See our Notice at Collection and
Privacy Policy at prh.com/notice.

Library of Congress Cataloging-in-Publication
Names: Hassan, Hawa, 1982– author. Title: Setting a place
for us: recipes and stories of displacement, resilience,
and community from eight countries impacted by war /
Hawa Hassan; location photography by Mahab Azizi, Riley
Dengler, Aline Deschamps, Doaa Elkady, Omer Khan,
Belal Mostamand, Somaya Samawi; food photography
by Julia Gartland. Identifiers: LCCN 2024025595 (print)
| LCCN 2024025596 (ebook) | ISBN 9781984860972
(hardcover) | ISBN 9781984860989 (ebook) Subjects:
LCSH: International cooking. | LCGFT: Cookbooks.
Classification: LCC TX725.A1 H3175 2025 (print) |LCC
TX725.A1 (ebook) | DDC 641.59—dc23/eng/20240729 LC
record available at https://lccn.loc.gov/2024025595 LC
ebook record available at https://lccn.loc.gov/2024025596

Hardcover ISBN: 978-1-9848-6097-2
Ebook ISBN: 978-1-9848-6098-9

Printed in China

Acquiring editor: Dervla Kelly
Co-project editor: Claire Yee
Production editor: Liana Faughnan
Editorial assistant: Gabby Ureña Matos
Designer: Isabelle Gioffredi
Art director: Emma Campion
Production designers: Mari Gill and Mara Gendell
Production manager: Serena Sigona
Prepress color manager: Jane Chinn
Travel producer: Kwame Apraku
Recipe developer: Amy Stevenson
Food stylist: Alya Hameedi
Copy editor: Sharon Silva
Proofreader: Nancy Inglis
Indexer: Elizabeth Parson
Publicist: Kristin Casemore
Marketer: Brianne Sperber

10 9 8 7 6 5 4 3 2 1

First Edition